WRITE THE VISION

See it! Say it! Step into what God promised!

DAILY AFFIRMATIONS FOR KINGDOM DREAMERS

VOLUME 1

COMPILED BY

KISHMA A. GEORGE

Write the Vision; See It! Say It! Step Into What God Promised!

Compiled by Dr. Kishma A. George

Published in the United States of America by

ChosenButterfly Publishing LLC

www.ChosenButterflyPublishing.com

ISBN: 978-1-945377-56-3

First Edition Printing

Printed in the United States of America

February 2026

Table of Contents

WRITE THE VISION

Welcome Letter from Apostle Dr. Kishma George

"Write the vision, and make it plain…" – Habakkuk 2:2

Greetings Dreamers,

Welcome to *Write the Vision, a divine* collection of affirmation statements, declarations, and prophetic insight birthed from the hearts of dreamers who dared to believe God's promises! This book is more than words on paper; it is a birthing room of destiny, a sacred space where faith meets action and vision comes alive.

When God spoke to the prophet Habakkuk, He gave a timeless instruction: *Write the vision and make it plain, so that he who reads it may run.* Every author within these pages has taken that command to heart. Through prayer, tears, and triumph, they have written visions that will inspire generations to come. Each affirmation is a declaration of faith, a reminder that what God has spoken will come to pass.

This book was designed to awaken the visionary within you. Whether you are at the beginning of your journey or standing on the threshold of manifestation, *Write the Vision* will stir your spirit to dream again, believe again, and run with renewed strength toward your God-given purpose.

As you read, I encourage you to speak each affirmation aloud, allowing the words to breathe life into your atmosphere. Let these declarations shift your mindset, align your heart with Heaven's agenda, and empower you to manifest the vision that God placed within you before the foundation of the world.

Dreamers, this is your *kairos* moment, your appointed time to rise, create, and move in divine purpose. You are not here by accident. God has called you to be a carrier of light, a builder of destiny, and a voice of transformation in the earth. So take your pen, take your faith, and *write the vision* with boldness and clarity.

May every word in this book ignite your passion, strengthen your faith, and remind you that you are chosen to dream, design, and deliver God's vision on Earth.

Blessings,

Apostle Dr. Kishma George

www.kishmageorge.com

How to Use This Book

This book is more than something to read—it is meant to be **experienced**.

Each section is designed to guide you through a journey of identity, healing, vision, purpose, and legacy. There is no need to rush. Move through the affirmations at a pace that allows reflection, growth, and alignment with God.

Read one affirmation or chapter at a time, slowly and with intention. Whenever possible, speak the affirmations aloud. There is power in declaring truth, and hearing your own voice reinforces faith and focus.

After reading, pause and reflect. Consider what stands out and how it applies to your life in this season. You may find it helpful to journal your thoughts, prayers, or insights as you move through the book.

Return to this book as often as needed. These affirmations are meant to meet you where you are and to support you in living out what you declare each day.

Identity & Foundation

Who You Are in God

Before you speak it, build it, or pursue it, you must **know who you are**.

This section anchors you in truth, reminding you that your worth, strength, and calling were established by God before you ever took your first step. These affirmations ground you in identity, silence doubt, and give you permission to walk boldly as who God created you to be.

Love, Light and Life with Jesus

Affirmations by Evangelist Julia Melissa Pierre

Declare: As a reflection of illuminating responsibility and integrity to myself and others I will be true and accountable to biblical values and principles. I believe through Jesus Christ you have no limits as to what you can achieve

I Give Myself Permission to Shine!

Permission to Shine

Psalm 16:11 KJV: Thou wilt shew me the path of life: In thy presence is fulness of joy; At thy right hand there are pleasures for evermore.

Permission to shine is the journey to divine purpose. We are up for the task to be the reflection of our illuminating self. God will keep moving in love, wisdom, and authority for those who have allowed themselves to experience the fullness of His joy. Bring the Word of God to life knowing that nothing is impossible for those who trust in the Lord. We have permission to shine in our authentic core living the purpose of God's glory, divine illumination, and the righteous living out of our faith.

"Let your light shine before others"

Matthew 5:16 (KJV): Let your light so shine before men, that they may see your good works, and glorify your Father which is in heaven.

God has blessed us. We have been trained and processed to move full throttle into the work and assignments of our life's purpose locked and loaded for the world shift, sharing in Yeshua's affections through afflictions for His Church, the Body's Kingdom mindset.

For fellowship to increase in our hearts, minds, and valued efforts we must encourage our inner wisdom, passion, and drive for living, loving and light, seeking and living a Kingdom lifestyle, sharing and caring with intentionally, applying Kingdom principles in our lives through faith, grace and vision. We must accept God's commission to become a servant and make His Word fully known in the ages and generations coming to reveal the mysteries of God revealed through His saints.

Matthew 13:43: Then the righteous will shine forth like the sun in the Kingdom of their Father

Focus on the journey to divine purpose and a spirit-filled connection that resonates the truth and strives to be filled with the knowledge of God that the masses in all wisdom and spiritual understanding will manifest a life and vision so that we may walk worthy of the Lord. My natural gifts are overflowing with my Spiritual calling to bear fruit and blooming knowledge of the Lord's Love, Light and Life. I'm compelled to birth and encourage many to embrace their spiritual purpose to make sense of their natural existence. My/Our Light is evidence of goodness, righteousness, and truth that God expects me to live wisely. The keys to live accountably, accepting the command to be continually filled with the Holy Spirit, helping and assisting others to gain a clearer insight into studying and applying the instructions and principles of the Word of God. **I pray many view their gifts and talents as a way to living a more balanced and fulfilling life by embracing Christ**.

Isaiah 60:1: Arise, shine, for your light has come

I desire for true Kingdom living and lifestyle. Living the biblical lifestyle God designed and prepared for the world. Living on purpose as God intended… kingdom principles that when applied to life circumstances actually work. Teaching others to learn, understand and apply wisdom for daily living in these trying times and how to be equipped, locked and loaded.

Whenever the force of darkness keeps us dead to sin from living in abundance, freedom and unavailability to the Jesus that lives in us, the fullness of life is found in the Love of Jesus. **Ephesians 3:19 KJV [19]:And to know the love of Christ, which passeth knowledge, that ye might be filled with all the fulness of God**

Every encounter is a Christ-centered encounter. Never to carry the burden of needs for others. Colossians KJV 1:24–29 explains the nature of Christian ministry, highlighting that Paul, despite suffering, rejoices as a steward of God's grace to bring the mystery of Christ to the world. BEWARE of those who resist the will of God for they too will resist the truth you offer.

John 1:11 NIV He came to that which was his own, but his own did not receive him

God's glory, divine illumination, and abundant love empower righteous living.

Be grateful God chose us to express Him through us by giving Love, Light and Life to those around us.

Evangelist Julia Melissa Pierre

Evangelist Julia Melissa Pierre is directed by the Holy Spirit as a mother, grandmother, pastor, inner conflict resolution mediator, spiritual and natural doula, licensed Medicare insurance advocate, and business owner. She has fulfilled 30 years of ministry in many capacities. Internationally, she has been compelled to birth and encourage many to embrace spiritual purpose that enables their natural existence.

Julia has been ordained by the Apostolic anointing of Bishop James and Pastor Lisa Keys of Pennsylvania, affirmed by her spiritual grandfather Apostle Gilbert Coleman Jr. of Freedom Christian Bible Fellowship in Philadelphia PA.

She has been commissioned to birth and encourage many to embrace their spiritual purpose to make sense of their natural existence, assisting them to gain a clearer understanding by studying and applying the instructions and principles of the Word of God.

I Am Athletic

Affirmations by Princess Tonya D. Green Affiba

Dictionary.com defines the term athletic as physically strong, fit, and active. I will take it a step further to add that athletes are also mentally, emotionally, and spiritually strong, fit and active. Consider these variables as you join the ranks of our predecessors who pushed themselves to the limit to make an exceptional difference in life.

I am physically fit for the journey. In your strength I can crush an army; with my God I can scale any wall. (Psalm 18:29, NLT) It is essential to prepare our bodies for the journey that the Lord assigned to us to finish the race set before us. When I was in bootcamp, my drill instructors pushed my body to the max. To keep going, we would declare, "No pain, no gain." I did not recognize it then, but the strength-building taught me to surpass my limitations. The physical fitness workouts toned my body at the end of my training and I had more endurance than when I started. Whatever tasks were assigned to me in training or the field, I had the energy and physical capability to handle them. Our bodies are a necessity and not an option. Right now, declare, "I am physically fit for this journey!" Now, train your body.

I am mentally fit for the journey. Casting down arguments and every high thing that exalts itself against the knowledge of God, bringing every thought into captivity to the obedience of Christ. (II Corinthians 10:5, NKJV) Life has a way of branding events in your mind, good and bad. The good memories bring joy, peace, and a healthy outlook. The bad often cause us to doubt God, mark time, or retreat. The enemy uses this strategy against Believers to keep them from advancing the Kingdom and living a productive life. However, you have the mind of Christ! Christ overcame every temptation by first thinking on the words from the Father and then declaring and acting on those power-packed words. Even as you read this passage, consider your thoughts and every one that does not glorify God, exclaim, "I have the mind of Christ and every thought that does not glorify God is under arrest! I am mentally fit for this journey."

I am oratorically fit. For assuredly, I say to you, whoever says to this mountain, "Be removed and be cast into the sea," and does not doubt in his heart but believes that those things he says will be done, he will have whatever he says. (Mark 11:23, NKJV) Our words hold weight and direct the course of our lives. We can create or destroy with words. By the Word of the Lord, that which did not exist now exists. Learn to speak legally and intelligently. Consider the prophet Elijah, who caused it to rain by commanding the drought to end. Do not keep silent. Shout, "I am oratorically fit!"

I am emotionally fit. Yeshua declared, Father, if you are willing, please take this cup of suffering away from me. Yet I want your will to be done, not mine. (Luke 22:42, NLT) Yes, the Lord had emotions but did not allow his feelings to govern him. Negative emotions draw us away from things or people we sometimes should be navigating towards, even God Himself. They are also weapons in the hands of the enemy and cause us to shrink back. As we submit ourselves to the Lord and heal, we can bring our emotions under control and use them to glorify God. God's instructions should always govern us, not our emotions. It is pertinent to understand this because we may be asked to venture into territories or take on assignments that make us uncomfortable. Think about the garden scenario. What if Yeshua was driven by his emotions? There would never have been a victory at Calvary. Settle it now. Since life and death are in the power of the tongue and you will eat the fruit thereof, stand boldly in the mirror and declare, "I am emotionally fit for the assignment on my life! I have discipline over my feelings."

I am positionally fit. Therefore, if anyone is in Christ, he is a new creation; old things have passed away; behold, all things have become new. (II Corinthians 5:17, NKJV) Listen, you are on the winning team. The moment you became one with Christ, you positioned yourself to win! He came that we would have life more abundantly in him. Think about this. If a football player dressed in his uniform and sat on the bench, he won if his team won. Remind yourself daily, "I am in Christ, who has already overthrown the powers of darkness. Yes, I am positionally fit to excel."

I am more than a conqueror. Yet in all these things we are more than conquerors [Heb. Hupernikao] through Him who loved us. (Romans 8:37, NKJV) To conquer means to overcome by force and take control. I had to learn that Christ took the sting of death, hell, and the grave. He defeated the enemy first. So, what made me realize that I was more than a conqueror was that I was evicting an already defeated foe from my life. We are not contending with a force to overthrow him by our strength. No, we are the clean-up crew! Notice that it is not in our name that demons tremble and flee but the name of Yeshua. It is high time to exercise your sonship right to move obstacles out of your way and control your life's path. Back in the day, there was a saying, "work ain't hard." Get a picture of the obstacle you desire to abolish and with great authority announce, "I am more than a conqueror through Christ Jesus who loves me. Go now and do not return to my life anymore."

I am the winner. Do you not know that in a race all the runners run but only one receives the prize? Run in such a way as to take the prize. (I Corinthians 9:24, BSB) Faith comes by hearing. It amazes me how quick we are to advise others to keep them motivated and encouraged, yet we struggle to apply that advice to ourselves. I want you to know that you are a priority. Since you are athletic, I challenge you to beat your own record. Increase the number of times you call yourself a winner to three times daily. Make it five times if within your diurnal course situations arise that make you feel defeated.

Princess Tonya D. Green Affiba

Princess Tonya D. Green Affiba is the 2024 recipient of the Who's Who in America Award, coauthor of several best-selling books, and has been featured on the cover of several prominent magazines. She is a native of Baltimore, MD, has two children, Donte (Denaja) and Danielle, and six grandchildren. She is the founder of Women of Dominion International, LLC and overseer of Restoration Nation Embassies. Through these platforms she has trained many and led teams on the mission field where she recently constructed an orphanage in Africa called Affiba's House. Her love for travel motivated her to become the owner of Sfera Travels. She has traveled to more than 15 nations to carry the Good News. She endeavors to finish her course and keep the faith.

Contact Information:

Website: wodintl.org

Email: womenofdominion9@gmail.com

Facebook: WOD International, LLC

IG: twodinternational

Rumble: twodintlg

It's Not Too Late!

Affirmations by Gina C. Edwards

Regardless of your age or your season of life, know that it's not too late. God is a "now" God. "Now unto Him who is able to do exceedingly abundantly, above all that we ask or think (Ephesians 3:20); Now faith is the substance of things hoped for the evidence of things not seen (Hebrews 11;1); Now to Him who is able to keep you from stumbling (Jude 24); Until now you have not asked nothing in my name, ask and you will receive, that your joy may be full (John 16:24); Now may the Lord of peace Himself give you peace. (II Thessalonians 3:16)." God displays purpose in everything! What seemed like a delay to you, God turns it around for His glory and for your good. He knows how to redeem your times and restore what the enemy has stolen from you.

God always has an appointed time, a right now time. And your role is to believe! Your role is to trust God. Your role is to operate in faith, in the supernatural! And call those things that be not as they are … right into the now. Stop expecting delays. Stop delaying yourself through doubt and negative conversations, even negative conversations you have within yourself. You must ensure you are speaking life and the promises of God each day. Yes, it's okay to encourage yourself! Use these seven affirmations of faith to keep focused on things above the earth, not on the earth. These affirmations will prepare you for your future and command your present!

Affirmation Statement - I am fulfilling the purpose God has placed on my life, regardless of my age or circumstances.

Many times, we believe that we have nothing to offer because of our age or the season of life we are in. But that is not true. Yes, we have a responsibility to train the next generation, but that doesn't mean we are useless. I refuse to stop dreaming or pursuing my goals because I'm a GiGi (grandmother lol). Regardless of what season we are in (singleness, divorce, married, senior, millennial) it doesn't matter, we still have purpose. I will be intentional on completing God's will in the earth with authority and without apology. He has redeemed my times and restoration is my portion. That means nothing that has happened to me in the past that will hinder me. In fact, God will use every situation in my life and turn it around for my good and His glory.

I love the scripture, Jeremiah 29:11, "For I know the thoughts that I think toward you, says the Lord, thoughts of peace, and not of evil, to give you a future and a hope" (NKJV). The KJV says "to give you an expected end." That tells me that God has great things in store for you and you can't give up when things get rough. You have to keep pressing towards the mark. Remember, God is a forward moving God and He knows our end from the beginning. So, you can trust Him with all of your heart.

Affirmation Statement - I am walking by faith and will stand on the promises of God even if it doesn't make natural sense.

Hebrews 11:1 (AMP) "Now faith is the assurance (title deed, confirmation) of things hoped for (divinely guaranteed), and the evidence of things not seen (the conviction of their reality—faith comprehends as fact what cannot be experienced by the physical senses)."

We can be so engrossed in living with our natural sense that we have to remind ourselves that we are first spiritual beings and we must operate in the spirit not the flesh. Even our analytical minds can hinder us from walking by faith. Somehow, we think we can figure it all out and actually help God. We have to be cognizant that the foundation of our relationship with God started with faith and is sustained by faith. You see "Without faith it is impossible to please God" (Hebrews 11: 6). Furthermore, our faith will be challenged as we grow in our walk with God. Bottom line—do we trust God or ourselves more? Even when the natural elements say one thing, we have to go with the Word and the voice of God. It forces us to examine if we really believe that He will provide, protect, deliver, heal and hear our prayers.

If we don't, we can't move forward from the spot we are in. I admit that there are times when I really don't understand what God is doing and it can be frustrating. Then I have to remind myself that He alone is God, which means He is Omnipotent, Omnipresent and Omniscient. And knowing He loves me greater than I can imagine, I can trust He knows what's best for me. At that time, I then have to get out of my emotions, the anxiety, the worry, the stress and stand still. Psalms 46:10 in the NASB version is so clear:

"Cease striving and know that I am God." So be quiet, stop fussing and stop complaining. Amen!

Phil 4: 6 & 7 reminds us to "Be anxious for nothing, but in everything by prayer and supplication with thanksgiving, let your requests be made known to God. And the peace of God which surpasses all understanding will guard your hearts and minds through Christ Jesus." You have to get to the place called peace! You have to relinquish all of your cares, literally unto Him. And this, my sister, is the walk of faith and ultimately the walk of greatness!

Affirmation Statement - My life has been redeemed from my past and I will not sabotage myself.

One thing I learned about my past, I used to be an expert in hindering myself. All the enemy had to do was plant a negative seed of doubt or insecurity in my mind and I took it from there. I began questioning myself, rehearsing past hurts and poor decisions. Finally, I realized that I was stuck and not operating in faith. I was not aligning my life or mindset up with the Word of God. So, I had to find out what God said about me. Right! I found scriptures that confirmed my identity and meditated on them. Some of my favorites include: Psalms 139:13–18, Philippians 1:6, Ephesians 2:10 and Isaiah 61:1–3.

Speak prophetically to yourself. "Yes, I am a new creation in Christ. My past does not dictate to me anymore." You can proclaim that, "Although I'm not perfect, I am complete (Girl, this liberated me!)" Tell yourself, "I am a royal diadem in God's hand. I am a masterpiece created in God's image; therefore I am beautiful! Amen!"

Affirmation Statement - My steps are ordered by God; therefore, all things work together for my good.

I've often wondered how God will turn something around for my good. You see, when you are in the midst of trouble, you don't always see the light at the end of the tunnel. And sometimes it's hard to believe that God will deliver you and then work things out for your good, especially when you caused the problem. Most of the time we don't believe God has forgiven us and, worse than that, we don't forgive ourselves either. Therefore, when we hear that our steps are ordered by God that means He knows what our future holds. And yes, He will allow you to make mistakes and mess up. It's called "free will".

But through His loving grace and mercy, He doesn't hold our sin against us. When we confess our sins, He is faithful and just to forgive us of our sins and cleanse us from all unrighteousness (I John 1:9). When I was 19, I had an abortion. One of the hardest decisions of my life. Mind you, I was a preacher's kid and unmarried. It was truly a scary time for me. In fact, it took years for me to reconcile with what I did. All I felt was guilt and shame. I would say in my 30s, as I grew in the love of God and understood His mercy, I was able to receive God's forgiveness (even though it was always there). I was also able to release the guilt that hung over my head for years.

I encourage you today to release the mistakes and poor decisions you've made. Let them go! Then allow God to wash you and restore the beauty He created in you. Tell yourself, "My times are in God's hands. I walk with a sound mind, in peace. I am not confused or lost. I hear the voice of God and will operate in wisdom. God has begun a good work in me.

Affirmation Statement - I am living my life on purpose!

Let's first define what purpose means; it is "the reason something exists or being intentional." I have always believed that each of us has a purpose on this earth. God is an intentional God and creates with purpose in mind. However, I further believe that most people don't know what their purpose is or how to obtain it. Gratefully, God has shown us in His Word who we are—look at Philippians 1:6, Psalms 37:23 and Romans 12:4–8. Now, the Word doesn't explain each of our destinies in detail since we all have a different path, but it is clear that God created you as a "masterpiece" to fulfill His purpose in the earth. He has also given us natural clues as well. First think about what you enjoy doing, no matter how you think or feel, and what you would do for "free". Purpose is concealed in those areas.

I will say life is more fulfilling when you know you are living out your purpose. You find hope in each day and look forward to your next assignment. Since we are created in God's image, that makes us intentional beings too. That's why you have to write out the vision, so you don't lose focus for there are many distractions in the world. Be mindful that when you walk out your destiny, you are living a life of success for your purpose honors God and points people to His heart.

Purpose will bring you joy, favor, strength and peace. Walking in purpose means you are a problem solver, a generational curse breaker and an idea generator. I encourage you to do one thing each day that brings you a step closer to fulfilling your dreams or purpose.

Affirmation Statement - I walk in financial prosperity!

Financial freedom is our right as joint heirs with Christ. Believe me, I recognize that life can get rough and that we go through lean times, but we don't have to live there. God has equipped us to be able to create wealth. He has given each of us talents and gifts that can help support and fund our vision. And as we sow into the Kingdom of God, He promised to take care of us. Matthew 6:33 says, "But seek first the Kingdom of God and His righteousness and all of these other things will be added to us."

Therefore, we can proclaim that we have creative ideas and will create generational wealth for our families. We can declare that there is no lack in our lives for we have the ability to call things from Heaven to the earth. We live in God's economy! So no matter what is going on in the world, we can trust that God will take care of us. Remember our God will supply all of our needs, according to His riches in glory (Philippians 4:19). We just have to believe it!

Affirmation Statement - I am not walking in fear but with boldness.

Fear is a powerful emotion and can be a stronghold if not dealt with properly. It is used as a weapon from the enemy to hinder our purpose and walk with God. If you succumb to fear, you will not operate in faith and will be paralyzed or stuck from living out your life through Christ. Remember that we are new creations in Christ and victorious in this earth. The past doesn't have authority over you; neither do present circumstances that seem overwhelming. Philippians 4:13 says, "I can do all things through Christ who strengthens me." We can't do anything in our own strength, even if we think we can. But when you partner with Christ—nothing is impossible!

Faith without works is dead, so you have to step out of your comfort zone and operate in purpose. It doesn't matter how old you are and where you've come from. You can fulfill your destiny! Therefore, declare today, "I am not afraid to be who God created me to be. I will step out on faith for my destiny is connected to others. I will share my story so God is glorified and others are edified. I am a minister of reconciliation. I believe that I'm walking in divine success, through divine doors, with divine opportunities. I will not continue to miss opportunities out of self-doubt or fear. I am equipped for this journey!"

Elder Gina Edwards

Elder Gina Edwards is the Founder of I Am Royalty Ministries. I Am Royalty Ministries began in 2017 after Gina wrote her second book, *Unearthing the Royalty from Within.* Ministering to women has always been on Gina's heart and she openly uses her personal experiences to relate to women of all backgrounds. This ministry empowers and ministers to the whole woman: spiritually, emotionally and professionally. Her ministry takes place through empowering messages, books, conferences and workshops. The goal of I Am Royalty Ministries is to empower women to become their best selves and to fulfill their Godly purpose.

Gina published her first book, *Imparting Eternity*, in 2014. This book inspires the reader to discover their purpose and then impart into others through their unique gifts. Her second book, *Unearthing Your Royalty from Within*, came alive from her pageant days. Years after winning a pageant, Gina realized she did not value the queen that wore that beautiful crown. This book challenges you to uncover your own crown and journal your progress. Her most recent book is entitled *Refreshing* and was written in 2021. This book encourages leaders and workers in ministry to learn how to stop and refuel! It's important to be able to refresh yourself without feeling guilty. Gina is also a psalmist and a playwright of inspirational musical plays. She is currently working on her first CD release entitled "A Worship Experience!"

Gina is a member of Word Alive Worship Center, in New Castle, DE, under the leadership of Pastors Anthony and Glenda Bailey. Gina serves as an elder, instructor and as a worship leader. Her favorite scripture is Psalms 46:10: "Stand still and know that I am God!" This scripture reminds her to be still, listen and seek God.

Gina enjoys spending time with her family, traveling, going to the movies, reading and writing. She is known as GiGi to her three beautiful grandchildren. Professionally she works as a director of human resources for a Delaware law firm. She received her Bachelor of Arts Degree in Business Administration from California State University and obtained her Masters in Organizational Leadership at Wilmington University.

You can connect with Gina on her website: www.ginacedwards.com or on Facebook.

SPEAK IT!

Affirmations by Dr. Mary J. Huntley

Affirmation: I Live by Faith Daily

Words have power! That's why it is very important that I speak life and create my purposeful life according to Proverbs 18:21, which states that death and life are in the power of the tongue. Whatever I need, God has given me the authority through His Word to speak it into existence with my tongue, which is my creative force. Therefore, it is imperative that I speak positive affirmations daily. These affirmations help shape my environment as well as confirm my identity, my spiritual heritage. Lastly, these confirmations enable my inheritance to manifest on planet Earth where I can receive and enjoy them.

Hebrews 11, known as the "Hallmark of Faith," defines faith as the substance of things hoped for and the evidence of things not seen. Therefore, my faith must place a demand on heaven's supply until my inheritance manifests on planet Earth. I must confess and profess God's Word believing that I receive when I pray and it shall come to pass. I have history with God including present confidence based on past experience. He's not a man to lie; neither the son of man that he should repent. My focal point must be confessing His Word daily, remaining in a state of expectancy, and thanking Him for the manifestation. I must remember that He is faithful and continue to praise Him even before my blessing manifests. Three times in the scripture God says, "The Just Shall Live by Faith" (Heb. 10:38, Hab. 2:4, Romans 1:17 KJV). Sounds like God really wants me to get the message and live by faith; mustard-seed faith that depends on His finished works and what He's done for me. Matthew 9:29 (TPT Version) says "I will have what my faith expects."

Affirmation: I Am God's Masterpiece/Workmanship!

Ephesians 2:10 says, "For we are God's masterpiece" (NLT Version).

I am special, created from the best of the best and rolled out as a limited edition by my God. I am a limited edition because God only made one me and decided that was enough. My temperament is the inborn part of man that determines how I react to people, places, and things assigned uniquely to me. It's my spiritual DNA that God placed in me in my mother's womb and before I rolled off His assembly line. Now that is definitely special! Extraordinary skills are required to create a masterpiece. Not ordinary but over-the-top skills were utilized when God created me. I am created in His image and after His likeness. When He created me, He said that it was very good.

"For we are his workmanship…" Ephesians 2:10 (KJV)

The transforming power of the Lord Jesus Christ saturates every fiber of my being. It's no more I but the Christ in me. In the mind of God, when Christ was crucified on the cross, I was crucified with Him. When He was buried, the old me was buried with Him. When He got up, I got up, and now I'm seated with Him in heavenly places. I have been empowered to get up from anything that tries to hold me back because greater is He that's in me than he that's in the world. So, when you look at me, you're looking at a dead person walking. The scripture says, reckon yourselves to be dead. My friends may ask me, "What happened to the old you?" I simply tell them she no longer exists.

Affirmation: I Am Chosen!

God doesn't just love me, but His agape (unconditional) love for me allowed Him to choose me to be included in His royal family. He didn't send Gabrielle, Michael or any other angelic being to choose me; but he hand-picked me (John 15:16 KJV). Though He knows my faults, failures, and flaws, He still chose me. He knew that I was not perfect, but He still chose me. He knew that He could use me once I received His only begotten son Jesus as my Savior and Lord. Once I received salvation through His son, He knew that, like Paul, I would pivot and do great exploits for the Kingdom. I would no longer live to serve and please the enemy, but I would actually change my abode and become a Kingdom ambassador. I would trust in the Lord with all of my heart and lean not unto my own understanding. I would acknowledge God in all my ways and allow Him to direct my path. Whatever challenges I face daily, I cast the care upon God knowing that He cares for me. He is my Jehovah-Jireh, my constant nourisher and provider.

Today, I am blessed and honored to have been chosen by God as one of His children. It is my distinct privilege and pleasure to represent my Father God in a spirit of excellence and bring Him all well-deserved glory. I'm grateful that He thought that I was worth saving, so Christ died on Calvary where my sins were forever nailed. And because I accepted His son as my Savior, I am blessed and privileged to say, "I am redeemed." I have been bought back and brought back into a right relationship with God because I am chosen. Thank you, Jesus! Glory to God!

Affirmation: I am Royalty! I Have Been Adopted into the Royal Family!

1 Peter 2:9 confirms my royalty: "But ye are a … royal priesthood." And this establishes a very important part of my identity. My Father God is the King of kings who adopted me into the royal family. Glory to God! I do not have to live like a second-class citizen because I am royalty. My Father God owns everything. He owns the best and I am grateful. I don't have to beg Him to provide for me. But it is His good pleasure to take care of me. And I thank Him daily. God chose me in spite of all of my flaws, failures, and imperfections to be adopted into his family "having predestinated us unto the adoption of children by Jesus Christ to himself, according to the good pleasure of his will," (Ephesians 1:5KJV). Once I received his only begotten son as my Savior and the Lord of my life, I became royalty. I have also been given certain rights and privileges of the Kingdom. What an awesome blessing! The Holy Spirit leads and guides me and shows me things to come. My Father God has given His angels charge over me to keep me in all my ways. My angels are so attentive to me that they bear me up in their hands even before I dash my foot against a stone. What awesome protection!

Affirmation: I Am More Than a Conqueror!

When babies are born, they are usually fed baby formula because of their age. As a newborn babe in Christ, I had to desire the sincere milk of the Word until I was strong enough to eat spiritual meat. My spiritual diet included reading and studying God's Word so that I could apply it to my daily life. Later, I enrolled in a Christian Bible college to glean even more of the Word so that I could grow more. During my Bible classes I discovered in Christology that I didn't have a great high priest who could not be touched with the feelings of my infirmities. In essence, He cares about the smallest obstacle that tries to encroach upon my territory. Therefore, He left explicit directions in Romans 8:37 to remind me of my spiritual authority as a conqueror: "I am more than a conqueror through Jesus Christ." So, I don't have to put up with the enemy when he comes to steal, kill and destroy my property and my legacy. I reach into my spiritual arsenal, apply God's Word by faith, and speak to the mountain. And according to St Mark 11:23–24, the mountain has to move in Jesus' name. That is how I conqueror the enemy's territory—with God's Word. And as a result, I am more than a conqueror through Christ Jesus who loves me as stated in Romans 8:37.

Affirmation: I Am a Citizen of Heaven!

As a citizen of heaven, I am privy to have a sneak preview of amazingly beautiful coming attractions. Heaven can be described as a place where the streets are paved with gold; there will be no need for hospitals, morgues, cemeteries, doctors, and so much more. There will be no need for mortgage payments or property taxes, though I will have a mansion! There will be no need to be concerned with the electric bill or any other bills. How awesome! Heaven has more supplies than demands, nothing missing, nothing broken and no lack. That statement can be unsettling for some; but I look forward to seeing my Savior and the beauty of "the city." "But we are citizens of heaven, where the Lord Jesus Christ lives. And we are eagerly waiting for him to return as our Savior" (Philippians 3:20NLT).

Affirmation: I Am Healed!

The Bible states in Isaiah 53:5, "But he was wounded for our transgressions, he was bruised for our iniquities: the chastisement of our peace was upon him; and with his stripes we are healed" (KJV). Jesus went to Calvary, was beaten with a cat of nine tails, pierced in his side, had a crown of thorns placed on his head and was spat on to pay a debt that I could not pay. Once my debt was paid at Calvary sickness had no legal right to try to encroach upon my territory at any time. However, I know that the enemy comes to steal, kill, and destroy anything that he can, so I must believe and confess the Word for it to work. And I must remember that as a child of God, healing belongs to me. III John 2 says, "Beloved, I wish above all that you prosper and be in health even as your soul prospers." I am thoroughly convinced that it is God's will for His children to be well and bring him glory. Therefore, I must hold fast to my confession and my profession for God's Word to maintain my healing.

Dr. Mary J. Huntley

Dr. Mary J. Huntley, a.k.a. "Modern Day Harriet Tubman", is called to serve the hurting, rejected, unnoticed, and overlooked. She is on assignment to free them from the chains that enslave their minds as she empowers them by raising low self-esteem and teaching them that you can live amid poverty and possess a rich mentality that provides an escape route. She serves as a servant leader in her 501 (c)(3) organization. She is a multi-award winner inclusive of the Indy Author Legacy Award. She is also an official presenter of the Presidential Lifetime Achievement Award as well as a recipient of this prestigious award. Dr. Huntley is the blessed and grateful recipient of an earned Ph.D. and D. Min. Degrees. She has various titles and serves in several capacities including CEO and licensed professional counselor with 10 advanced certifications. She is a certified international speaker, multi-award winner and multi-international best-selling author, board-certified master mental health professional and board-certified master life coach. She is grateful and godly proud that her recent anthology, *Trust*

the Process: Reap The Harvest, became an international bestseller in several categories and countries and her inaugural solo project, "Don't Quit: Motivation To Reach Your Goals", sold in Antigua, Canada, and the UK and continues to motivate and inspire families around the world.

As a board-certified master mental health professional, she was blessed and grateful to serve as moderator (in conjunction with another mental health professional) of the Professional Mental Health Series, a community giveback program provided through her 501 (c)(3) organization, which addresses the global mental health crisis. The series provides a professional platform to help remove mental health stigmas one mind at a time. Additionally, she also sponsored a SOLD-OUT mental health summit. Through her non-profit organization she provides professional pro bono counseling and professional pro bono mental health coaching, mentoring and support for doctoral candidates, provides emergency funding for seniors, provides holiday meals, scholarships for summer camp and so much more to the community. Lastly, she serves as an international representative and clinical supervisor for a counseling organization.

She served as a strategic partner and sponsor in support of the SOLD-OUT Leadership Summit. Seasoned leaders, aspiring leaders, and entrepreneurs came from near and far to support this phenomenal event. Impactful panelists shared informative and impactful information to enhance business acumen and entrepreneurship. An awesome time was had by all. Dr. Huntley received Maryland Governor Wes Moore's Citation for demonstration of high integrity and ability, leadership, community services and contributions.

Affectionately known as the Master Motivational Mindset Coach she motivates, captivates, and elevates as she distributes high-octane motivation®. She has been featured on various billboards, most recently New York Times Square as "Top 10 Influential Relentless Women on the Move" and on "Powerless to Powerful Australian Podcast". She has been featured in *Brainz Magazine*, *VIP Global Magazine*, *Faith Heart International Magazine*, *Glambitious Magazine Voyage Atl*, *Bold Journey Magazine*, *UPWORD Global Magazine*, and Making Headline News, Radio One, ACTS Radio in London, and Impact the World Radio (VOXWAV). Her narrative and remarkable, unwavering mustard seed faith in God will unequivocally motivate you to rise up, speak up and follow up! She takes great pleasure in empowering others inclusive of assisting them to become international best-selling authors. One of her favorite mantras is "If serving is beneath me then leadership surely is beyond me." She is the grateful and blessed wife of fifty-one years to Dr. Ronald Lee Huntley. TO GOD BE ALL THE GLORY!

LET'S CONNECT

Facebook—DrMary J Huntley

Instagram—authordrmaryjhuntley

LINKEDIN—Dr. Mary J. Huntley

Healing & Renewal

Restoring the Mind and the Heart

Transformation begins within.

This section addresses the inner work—healing wounds, renewing the mind, releasing what no longer serves you, and strengthening your spirit. These affirmations guide you through restoration, resilience, and endurance so you are not merely surviving, but becoming whole.

Faith Focused to Lead in Ministry

Affirmations by Dr. Amicitia (Cita) Maloon-Gibson

Affirmation: I am loved and valued by God.

This affirmation is rooted in Psalm 139:13–14, which says God formed me in my mother's womb and I am fearfully and wonderfully made. This scripture highlights the intentional and personal nature of God's creation. Every detail of my existence, from my physical appearance to my personality and talents, is a result of God's deliberate craftsmanship. As a result, I am not an accident or a mistake but a masterpiece created with purpose and love. This truth can transform my self-perception and relationships, reminding me that my worth is not defined by external validation but by God's unwavering love. When I internalize this affirmation, I can live with confidence and security, knowing I am cherished and valued by my Creator.

Affirmation: I am forgiven and free from guilt.

In 1 John 1:9, it says if we confess our sins, God is faithful and just to forgive us our sins and cleanse us from all unrighteousness. This affirmation speaks to the liberating power of God's forgiveness. When I confess my sins, I am not only forgiven but also cleansed, freed from the weight of guilt and shame that can hold me captive. This truth allows me to confront my mistakes and weaknesses without being defined by them. By embracing God's forgiveness, I can experience emotional healing and release, walking in the freedom of a new life in Christ. This affirmation empowers me to live without the burden of past mistakes, embracing a future filled with hope and possibility.

Affirmation: I am strong and capable through God's power.

Philippians 4:13 says I can do all things through Christ who strengthens me. This affirmation is a declaration of faith in God's empowering presence. It's not about my own abilities or strengths but about the limitless power of God working through me. When faced with challenges or obstacles, I can draw on this divine strength, trusting that God will provide the resources and resilience I need to overcome them. This truth can transform my approach to difficulties, shifting my focus from my limitations to God's limitless potential. By leaning on God's power, I can accomplish far more than I ever thought possible, achieving victories that bring glory to God.

Affirmation: I am not anxious or worried.

Philippians 4:6–7 tells us to bring our concerns to God with thanksgiving and gratitude and His peace will guard our hearts and minds. This affirmation speaks to the peace that surpasses human understanding, available to those who trust in God. When worries and fears arise, I can turn to God in prayer, presenting my concerns and receiving His peace in return. This peace is not just the absence of anxiety but a positive, supernatural calm that permeates my entire being. By practicing this affirmation, I can experience a profound sense of tranquility, even in turbulent times, knowing that God is sovereign over all circumstances.

Affirmation: I am worthy and enough.

In 2 Corinthians 12:9, God's power is made perfect in my weakness, and His grace is sufficient for me. This affirmation highlights the paradox of spiritual strength, where my inadequacies become opportunities for God's power to shine. I don't have to be self-sufficient or perfect to be worthy; instead, my worth is rooted in God's unconditional love and acceptance. When I acknowledge my weaknesses and limitations, I can experience the empowerment of God's grace, which is always sufficient for every challenge. This truth frees me from the pressure to perform or achieve perfection, allowing me to rest in God's love and acceptance.

Affirmation: I am guided and led by God.

Proverbs 3:5–6 instructs us to trust in the Lord with all our heart and lean not on our own understanding and He will make our paths straight. This affirmation speaks to the guidance and direction available to those who trust in God. When I surrender my plans and decisions to God, I can experience His guidance and wisdom. This doesn't mean I'll always understand the path ahead, but I can trust that God is working everything out for my good. By embracing this affirmation, I can navigate life's complexities with confidence, knowing that God's guidance is available every step of the way.

Affirmation: I am blessed and chosen by God.

Ephesians 1:4 says God chose us in Christ before the foundation of the world to be holy and blameless in His sight. This affirmation highlights my identity as a beloved child of God, chosen and adopted into His family. I am not a random or accidental creation but a deliberately chosen and cherished child of the King. This truth can transform my self-perception and relationships, reminding me that my worth and identity are rooted in God's love. When I internalize this affirmation, I can live with confidence and purpose, knowing I am blessed and chosen for a life that brings glory to God.

Dr. Amicitia (Cita) Maloon-Gibson

Dr. Amicitia (Cita) Maloon-Gibson is a retired Lieutenant Colonel of the United States Army, having served with honor and distinction both nationally and globally. Following her military career, she continued her service as a Senior Executive Leader, holding various leadership roles across agencies within the Department of Defense and serving on Boards of Directors.

Dr. Gibson is the Founder of ATIC and MGAA Professional Development, organizations rooted in her vision of growing and empowering future leaders. Her professional credentials are extensive, including Professional Certified Speaker, Trainer, Executive Consultant, and Amazon Author. Known as *EmpowermentDoc*™, she inspires, leads, and equips others to become the best version of themselves.

Ordained in 2005 as an Evangelist and Servant Leader by the late Bishop Thomas Solomon, Dr. Gibson is a devoted woman of faith who stands firmly on God's Word, particularly Psalm 23 and Psalm 121. She is a lifelong learner who believes that true living is found in giving and intentionally investing in the next generation of leaders.

Facebook: https://www.facebook.com/AmicitiaMaloonGibson

Email: drcita@citagibson.com

Website: www.EmpowermentDoc.com

Renewing Your Mind with RAS Recode

Affirmations by Dr. Tavis Taylor

Introduction

The mind is the battlefield where victories are won or lost. Scripture tells us, "As a man thinketh in his heart, so is he" (Proverbs 23:7, KJV). The thoughts we dwell on shape our emotions, our choices, and ultimately our destiny. God has given us the ability to renew our minds, not by sheer willpower but by aligning our thoughts with His Word and promises. The Reticular Activating System (RAS) is a God-designed filter in the brain that plays a role in this renewal. What we focus on repeatedly our RAS highlights and reinforces. By confessing affirmations rooted in Scripture, we reprogram our mental filter to recognize God's truth, peace, and direction in everyday life. This chapter provides seven affirmations to help you train your RAS, align your thinking with God's truth, and step into transformation.

I set my mind on what is true, noble, and worthy of praise.

The Apostle Paul instructed us in Philippians 4:8 (NIV) to think on things that are true, noble, right, pure, lovely, admirable, excellent, or praiseworthy. Your Reticular Activating System (RAS) filters what you focus on. If you continually rehearse worry or negativity, your brain magnifies it. But when you train your RAS to dwell on truth and God's promises, you begin to see His goodness everywhere. Declare this affirmation daily to redirect your mental focus, reminding your mind that you choose what you magnify.

I am transformed as I renew my mind with God's Word.

Romans 12:2 (KJV) teaches, "Be ye transformed by the renewing of your mind." Transformation begins in the thought life. Your RAS responds to repeated declarations, creating new pathways of faith and courage. By confessing this affirmation, you partner with the Spirit to replace old patterns with God's truth. This shift doesn't happen overnight, but consistent practice brings lasting renewal.

I reject fear and align my mind with God's perfect peace.

Isaiah 26:3 (NIV) promises, "You will keep in perfect peace those whose minds are steadfast, because they trust in you." Fear is loud, but peace is steady. Training your RAS to recognize God's peace means teaching your brain to default to calm when life feels chaotic. Each time fear rises, affirm peace and watch how your mind begins to anchor itself in His presence.

I choose to replace lies with the truth of who I am in Christ.

The enemy's strongest weapon is deception. Yet John 8:32 (NIV) declares, "Then you will know the truth and the truth will set you free." When you confess this affirmation, your RAS begins to recognize lies for what they are and filter them out. It trains your subconscious to elevate God's Word above internal doubts or external criticism.

My thoughts align with God's plans to prosper me and give me hope.

Jeremiah 29:11 (NIV) affirms God's heart toward His people: "For I know the plans I have for you … plans to prosper you and not to harm you." By repeating this affirmation, your RAS becomes attuned to opportunities, resources, and connections that reflect God's good intentions for your life. Instead of expecting defeat, you begin to anticipate blessing.

I capture every thought and make it obedient to Christ.

2 Corinthians 10:5 (NIV) instructs us to "take captive every thought to make it obedient to Christ." Your mind often runs on autopilot, but your RAS can be retrained to reject unhelpful patterns. By affirming this daily, you remind yourself that you have authority through Christ to discipline your thinking. This is spiritual warfare fought in the mind, with victory secured by Christ.

My mind is fertile ground for God's Word to bear fruit.

Jesus taught in Matthew 13 (NIV) that the seed falls on different kinds of ground. When your RAS is cluttered with distractions, the Word can feel choked. But when you declare this affirmation, you're choosing to cultivate fertile soil in your mind. You are training your inner filter to highlight God's Word over competing noise, ensuring His promises grow and multiply in your life.

Conclusion

Renewing your mind is not a one-time event; it is a daily practice of replacing lies with truth, fear with faith, and chaos with peace. When you speak these affirmations consistently, you are retraining your RAS to highlight God's promises over life's pressures. Over time, you'll notice your perspective shifting, your faith growing stronger, and your ability to recognize God's hand in every detail of your life strengthening. As Paul reminds us, "We have the mind of Christ" (1 Corinthians 2:16, NIV). This means you already carry access to wisdom, clarity, and power. Keep rehearsing these truths until they become your default way of thinking. Your renewed mind will not only transform your own life but will also inspire those around you to believe for more.

Dr. Tavis Taylor

Dr. Tavis Taylor is a coach, pastor, and thought leader known as *The Digital Midwife*. As an AI consultant, she helps visionaries birth their God-given dreams through the integration of faith, neuroscience, and AI-powered tools. As the founder of **Emerentias**, she equips leaders, churches, and entrepreneurs to rewire their minds, embrace innovation, and build Kingdom-centered influence in a digital age.

Dr.Tavis's Acknowledgments

I thank God for revealing the power of a renewed mind and for entrusting me with the responsibility to share His truth. I also honor the visionaries and leaders who continue to inspire me to merge faith, neuroscience, and innovation for Kingdom impact. I would also like to thank Dr. Kishma George for this opportunity.

Morning D.E.W. (Daily Encouraging Words)

Affirmations by Danielle N. Hall

I speak what I seek until I see what I say.

Proverbs 18:20–21 (AMP) states, *"A man's stomach will be satisfied with the fruit of his mouth; He will be satisfied with the consequence of his words. Death and life are in the power of the tongue, and those who love it and indulge it will eat its fruit and bear the consequences of their words."* In other words, our words are seeds that will yield a fruit that we will one day have to partake in. I am allergic to lemons, so I avoid sour talk. While being mindful to avoid what we don't want to manifest in our lives by the words we speak, it is equally wise to sow seeds that we do pleasantly anticipate the harvest of. The Bible tells us in Matthew 6:33 that our primary seek should be the Kingdom and His righteousness. God's way comes first. All other things and matters are secondary. Once we take care of first things first, we find that our ask and our seek align with what He sees for our lives. What you see now may not look like promise, but God keeps His promises and if He has declared it, then there shall be a performance. God has already established your journey and your destiny. Align your words with His will and experience a harvest of plenty.

I maintain a heart of gratitude.

One definition of gratitude is heartfelt appreciation for the benefits and kindness received. Psalm 103:1–5 (AMP) says, *"Bless and affectionately praise the Lord, O my soul, and all that is [deep] within me, bless His holy name. Bless and affectionately praise the Lord , O my soul, And do not forget any of His benefits; Who forgives all your sins, Who heals all your diseases; Who redeems your life from the pit, Who crowns you [lavishly] with lovingkindness and tender mercy; Who satisfies your years with good things, So that your youth is renewed like the [soaring] eagle."* Psalm 63:3 (AMP) reads, "*Because Your lovingkindness is better than life, My lips shall praise You.*" With all these benefits available and the better-than-life lovingkindness, my posture can be nothing but gratitude. Furthermore, being grateful is a biblical command. We are admonished in 1 Thessalonians 5 to give thanks in every situation and in any circumstance because that's His will. We may not be grateful FOR what we are going through, but we can be grateful IN what we are going through because we don't walk alone. Our heavenly Father is very present. What I have experienced in my journey as a Believer is that gratitude does two things: it keeps you grounded and shifts your atmosphere. Complaining came with the consequences of anxiety, stress, depression, muscle tension, headaches and even the feeling of suffocation. As I grew, I realized that the more I took note of the benefits and kindness of the Lord the more I saw clearly and changed my confession. I thank Him for healing me from asthma;

I thank Him from healing me from the effects of the trauma of having been sexually assaulted and abused; I thank Him for saving me from the pits of hell when I was deep in sin; I thank Him for His mercies that keep me from being consumed; I thank Him for satisfying my life with good things even though I may have to go through some rough patches. All things work together for my good, but most importantly they work together for the greater good. When I recall to my mind what He has done, it gives me hope. Suddenly, the language change causes relief of tension, anxiety, stress, and depression. My focal point shifts and so does my atmosphere. It is an atmosphere permeated with perfect peace.

I persevere even when adversity is present.

When learning how to crawl and then walk as a Believer, I was often challenged by one who should have been my biggest supporter. There were efforts to make me believe that the steps I had been taking were not ordered by the Lord; that, somehow, I either misconstrued the voice or misheard the instructions. I knew within that it was the Lord I heard, but every time I obeyed God it seemed as though I was getting attacked by one who vowed to do the opposite. I would seek the Lord in prayer to make sure I had heard correctly and walked obediently. His response to me was consistently the same three words: "Just keep going." Those words became my mantra and I learned to stand strong even when the adversary reared his ugly head using who was close to me. *"If thou faint in the day of adversity, thy strength is small"* according to Proverbs 24:10 (KJV). The enemy of our souls is also the enemy of our progress. We must decide that we won't allow an already defeated foe to make us feel defeated. Rest, but don't quit. You are equipped not only to finish but to finish strong!

I view life through a healed lens.

The unhealed often walk by feelings and not faith. The unhealed are often easily offended. The unhealed will sometimes bleed on whom they lead. The unhealed find difficulty in trusting others. In essence, being unhealed can negatively impact both personal and professional relationships, our mental health, and our overall well-being. While I now identify as an overcomer of sexual assault and abuse and even narcissistic abuse, there was once a time when I was unhealed. Yet, I said I was okay when I truly wasn't. It was my "little white lie". I viewed myself as unworthy because violators made me feel that way and the perpetrators said so. I was a victim and not a victor. I had been silenced by guilt and shame. Before, when I wrote, it was cathartic: it had become my therapy … my safe space. It was my voice when I was otherwise silenced. I would write "woe is me" poems and sad journal entries. The unhealed me had taken on the identity that was projected onto me. Eventually, as I began to walk closer to God, my scope changed. I saw what He saw: His handiwork. I understood David's confession in Psalm 139:13–14 (AMP): *"For You formed my innermost parts; You knit me [together] in my mother's womb. I will give thanks and praise to You, for I am fearfully and wonderfully made; Wonderful are Your works, and my soul knows it very well."* Embracing God's love for us and His truth concerning us transforms our hearts, clears our lenses, and elevates our perspective. I exchanged the lie of me being okay (when I wasn't) for the truth of His love demonstrated by His ultimate sacrifice. Now when I write, it is from the healed place and it is to encourage, enlighten and empower the reader. I had to see the me that He saw and walk in it before I could help anybody else.

I wisely steward my time, talent, and treasure.

It has not been difficult for me to give or to help others. My parents were excellent examples of selflessness. However, I had to learn the significance of obedient giving. This is an intentional type of giving that requires hearing from and following the voice of the Lord. It is my firm belief from experience that the hands of an obedient giver will not be empty. Here's what the Word says in Matthew 25:29 (AMP): *"For to everyone who has [and values his blessings and gifts from God, and has used them wisely], more will be given, and [he will be richly supplied so that] he will have an abundance; but from the one who does not have [because he has ignored or disregarded his blessings and gifts from God], even what he does have will be taken away."* God is gracious and has blessed us with the gift of time, spiritual gifts, and the gift of monetary resources. How we steward them determines the level of abundance of those resources. Because I freely release what the Lord requires of me, I make the bold declaration that I have what I need and then some. It is a faith statement based on biblical principle. When you sparingly sow, you sparingly reap. When you generously sow, you generously reap. My abundance is an overflow for those who are in lack. I will not hoard what He gave me to use to help.

I walk in the freedom of forgiveness.

When we consider how while we were yet sinners Christ died for us, it should compel our hearts to exercise forgiveness towards others. The Bible declares in 1 John 1:9 (AMP), *"If we [freely] admit that we have sinned and confess our sins, He is faithful and just [true to His own nature and promises] and will forgive our sins and cleanse us continually from all unrighteousness [our wrongdoing, everything not in conformity with His will and purpose]."* This forgiveness is not something that we earned but something that Christ freely gifted us with so that we would be free from the penalty of sin. Accepting Christ's finished work on the Cross as the grace gift that it is encourages us to be free from the things that make us captive. His forgiveness towards us makes us free and our forgiveness towards others makes us free. Holding on to past hurts, bitterness, resentment and anger hinders us from growing and being well. When we forgive, our spirits are strengthened, our souls are made well, our growth is encouraged, and our freedom is evident. The truth is sometimes we fail to forgive ourselves. We burden ourselves with guilt and shame; we set unrealistic expectations on ourselves and engage in negative self-talk. This is not the will of God for us and it is a destructive pattern that will land us in a place called bondage. His message in Jeremiah 29:11 (AMP) encourages the Believer: *"'For I know the plans and thoughts that I have for you,' says the Lord, 'plans for peace and well-being and not for disaster, to give you a future and a hope.'"* God does not want us to fail. He wants us to be free. One of the most profound words of encouragement I heard from a minister of the gospel before I had a healthy relationship with God was, "God has already forgiven you. You just haven't forgiven yourself." That was one of the most life-changing revelations I received and I can still hear them loudly in my ear even 20+ years later.

I dwell in the realm of possibility.

With all that we see between mainstream media and social media, it can be discouraging and disheartening at times. We take in information that can begin to diminish the voice of God in our lives or we see things that somehow lead us to comparison and then self-doubt. We must remember who we are in Him and that He has a specific purpose for each of our lives. Within our journey we may find that some resources dry up, we will experience the loss of people or things that we are most comfortable or are familiar with, and we may even endure physical challenges. Some of these things can be true at the same time. However, when the resources dry up, we must remember who the ultimate Source is. While loss hurts and sometimes can cut deeply, in Him we have a firm foundation and we can still stand. The enemy will lie to us to make us think we are bankrupt when we have been endowed with countless blessings and benefits and we have a heavenly Father who takes great care of His children. If he gets us to think that we are bankrupt, then we are less likely to make Kingdom deposits. He is a liar. The truth isn't in him. Through God's Word we are equipped and by His Spirit we are empowered to accomplish all that He has planned for us to do. We must be reminded of the God Who is at work in us and Who specializes in what others say is impossible. Philippians 4:13 (AMP) is a bold declaration: *"I can do all things [which He has called me to do] through Him who strengthens and empowers me [to fulfill His purpose—I am self-sufficient in Christ's sufficiency; I am ready for anything and equal to anything through Him who infuses me with inner strength and confident peace]."* That is good news!

Danielle N. Hall

Danielle N. Hall is a board-certified Christian counselor and mental health coach who is an advocate for all to recognize and achieve their divine purpose. Additionally, she is a licensed minister who is continually looking for ways to enlighten, to encourage, and to empower others through this journey called life. She is a sexual abuse overcomer and the visionary/founder of V.O.I.C.E. (Victorious Overcomers Inspiring Christian Empowerment), which is a ministry that services women who have been sexually assaulted or abused.

She is the sole author of her debut book *Dew Drops: Refreshing for the Soul*, her sophomore book Amazon #1 Bestseller *Dirty Little Secrets & The Little White Lie*, and her junior release *Grace to Endure: You Don't Know My Story*. Danielle has been a contributing author of six projects: *She Wouldn't Let Me Fall* (2018), *Hope for the Overcomer's Soul* (2018), *My Whole Self Matters Empowerment Journey Journal* (2019), *My Praise Is My Weapon* (2020), *God Blocked It* (2023), and *Occupy* (2025). Additionally, Danielle presented her first book collaboration *The Heart That Forgives* in 2023. She is a budding entrepreneur and is the owner of both SOL by Danielle (a greeting card service launched in 2017) and The Butterfly Effect by Danielle (a butterfly-themed jewelry company launched in August 2019). In May 2023, Danielle launched The R.O.P.E., LLC (The Realm of Possibility Experience) where she employs her skillset as a coach and counselor. Previously widowed, she is a recently married mother of three who endeavors to both achieve and maintain balance given the demands of family, work, ministry, and self.

Danielle's Acknowledgments

I would like to thank Dr. Kishma George for her consistent Kingdom contributions and for the opportunity to participate in this empowerment project. I give thanks to my loving husband for his unending support. Lastly, I would like to thank God for salvation, preservation and transformation.

My Resiliency Won't Allow Me to Stay Down!

Affirmations by LeTonya Hudson

Affirmation: I will not bow to fear because my faith was built for the fire.

Faith doesn't exempt us from trials; it empowers us to walk through them unshaken. It gives us the shakable belief that we will not burn in the furnace. I say shakable because, although we have faith God will intervene, the human side tries to test us and can at times seem as if it has won. What we do know in those moments is resilience is found in knowing that even in the flames, God is present, protective, and powerful. He has the situation under control, just as He did with Shadrach, Meshach, and Abednego in Daniel 3:17–26 (KJV). I can walk through the situation(s) barely scorched by the heat! Resilience is found in knowing that even in the flames, God is present, protective, and powerful. "*When you walk through the fire, you will not be burned; the flames will not set you ablaze.*" Isaiah 43:2 (NIV)

Affirmation: I refuse to surrender my calling just because the path feels unfamiliar.

When God calls me, He equips me, even if the route is uncomfortable or unclear. In order to become the person I was designed to be, I had to go through many furnace fires, not only to grow my faith and dependence on the Father but also to have an undeniable testimony of the Grace He provides to us all. Real empowerment means trusting the voice of God over the volume of my fears, knowing that my obedience will open the door for breakthrough. The tests develop the testimony and I have been commissioned to share the Glory, Grace, and deep eternal Love God has for ALL His children. At times the vision may seem blurry and I do not know which path to choose. Those are the times I have to step aside and allow God to be God and I have to trust and listen to His instructions to get on the path He knows will lead me to safety and certainty to complete my assigned tasks. *"The one who calls you is faithful, and He will do it."* I Thessalonians 5:24 (NIV)

Affirmation: I rise today because God didn't bring me this far just to leave me here.

Resilience means rejecting the lie that this is where it ends. When I feel abandoned or tired, I lean into the promise that God's plan includes my comeback and the next chapter will carry His glory. As life keeps going forward, so do the stories of our lives. At times there are crossroads that must be addressed. These are obstacles that seem immovable while I am going through the situation(s). Naturally some are more complex than others, such as dealing with breast cancer, not once, but twice, in the same breast, pretty close to where it was the first time. Through self-exams, I was fortunate to find the small lump in its early stage both times. The first case was pretty standard and God was totally in control and walked me through that situation with minor pains and restrictions. The second case developed ten years later and many changes were made in the handling of treatment, the medicines are more advanced, but chemotherapy is still tiring. Life, physically, mentally and emotionally, changed the most. Harder decisions had to be made prior to surgery; after surgery a different set of thoughts had to be dealt with. I have been blessed beyond measure to have such a group (tribe) of God-fearing, praying, and warring women. I don't know what my full purpose is; I do know it's not complete because, by Grace, I am still here to fight the good fight … in Jesus' Name, Amen. *"Being strengthened with all power according to his glorious might so that you may have great endurance and patience."* Colossians 1:11 (NIV)

Affirmation: I walk in authority because I've survived what was meant to destroy me.

I carry weight because I've endured warfare. What was designed to take me out became the very foundation for my power and now I step boldly into purpose, clothed in divine confidence. I carry the knowledge that God continues to supply what I need in order to work out the purpose He designed just for me. I seek deeper understanding from His Word and do my best to please Him daily. It can be a tedious duty on some of those hard days when my mind and emotions attempt to take over and the enemy tries to test me. I just remind him and myself that I've been through tough storms, so small raindrops are just that! I continuously give God the praise because He is the only one to supply the strength I need to go another day! Thank You, Father! I have a mission to complete! *"No weapon forged against you will prevail, and you will refute every tongue that accuses you."* Isaiah 54:17 (NIV)

Affirmation: I stand tall because Grace refused to let me stay buried.

There were moments when I didn't think I'd make it, but Grace kept reaching for me. God's mercy didn't just pull me out; it lifted me higher and placed new strength beneath my feet. I don't have as many fearful moments as I did before. The Lord has never let me down and He forgives me every time I try to go around His Word. There may be some teachable moments attached, but I always give repentance because my way wasn't as good as I thought! I have a voice that will be heard; I have stories that must be told, all about how good my God has been to me! When I fall, it's a "whoop." Should I decide to stay down it would be an "oh-oh!" that I just cannot do. I must get up, brush myself off and say, "Okay God, I'm ready to continue on!"

"But you, Lord, are a shield around me, my glory, the One who lifts my head high." Psalm 3:3 (NIV)

Affirmation: I speak life over my future because I serve a God who restores what was lost.

Loss is not the end of my story. With God, every ruined season has the potential to be rebuilt with beauty and my words must align with His truth, not my past pain. We all have a story to tell about how good God has been in all facets of our lives. He never leaves us. He is omnipresent and will wait for us to remember who He is and how good He has been over our lives in ways that may have us forget it was Him that got us through. I look over my life and know that God has been with me in every situation, either helping me get through it or teaching me to depend on Him when I think I know what I'm doing! Just like a Father, He wants the best for me and I want to please Him. Yes, I still make mistakes and occasionally have fleeting thoughts of why or how a situation has temporarily taken over my life. God is patient and willing to wait until I have a talk with Him about how I'm feeling and why; afterwards, I thank Him for never leaving me and providing another chance. *"I will repay you for the years the locusts have eaten…"* Joel 2:25 (NIV)

Affirmation: I move forward boldly, knowing my story carries healing for others.

I didn't survive all that I have by accident; my breakthrough is someone else's blueprint. God anoints those who have endured with a mantle of restoration and my resilience becomes a testimony that shatters strongholds. I grew (and am still growing) my relationship with the Lord. I've always had casual prayers of gratitude, but I get in His Word more so I can truly understand Him and why I am so important to Him. He made me who I am and I am so appreciative, but I look at some major mistakes I made in my younger life and ask myself how He could continue to love me! Well, I am part of His creation; part of His legacy, part of His promises … for this I am grateful and when things get tough, I reach into my resilience toolkit and give Him all I can give, and pray for strength in order to be able to give Him more. For me, I am to move mountains and I still don't know how I will do it, but through Him, I will succeed. Trust the Father and give Him all you can give because that is exactly what He did for all of us! We can move mountains together and kick the enemy in the face! God is able! He made us able to do so.

"He comforts us in all our troubles, so that we can comfort those in any trouble..." II Corinthians 1:4 (NIV)

LeTonya M. Hudson

I'm LeTonya M. Hudson and I know what it means to lead through chaos. When life hits hardest, I've learned to respond not with panic but with purpose. My journey has taught me that every disruption holds the seed of strength. Whether I'm facing a turning point or trying to hold everything together for the sake of others, I write to remind you that you are not alone and you can rise from it, stronger and more determined than ever. As a proud "glamma" I know what legacy means; as a care provider I know what being resilient means; as an author I believe I have the words to make a change in the lives of others; as a speaker I know my voice was meant to be heard; as an advocate I know what servitude means; as a good friend and confidante to those who embrace and trust me with all their secrets, I try my best never to let them down; as a child of God, I know I could not be or do any of these things without the Hand of God over my life.

{**lemhudson@gmail.com**}

Empowered to Endure: End Times

Affirmations by Dr. Radiance L. Rose

I am fearfully and wonderfully made, created with divine purpose.

Scripture: *"I will praise You, for I am fearfully and wonderfully made; marvelous are Your works, and that my soul knows very well." – Psalm 139:14 (NKJV)*

Devotional Reflection:

As *artificial intelligence* advances, humanity is redefining identity through technology, algorithms, and virtual approval. Yet none of these can determine your worth. God's Word anchors you in eternal truth: you are His handcrafted creation, designed with divine intention. No machine can replicate the eternal imprint of God on your life. You were born into this generation to shine His light and live authentically in a culture of imitation. As the end approaches, remember—your purpose is not artificial; it is eternal.

Reflection Question: How can I embrace my God-given identity instead of conforming to digital standards of worth?

____

____

____

____

____

Prayer: Father, thank you for making me unique. Guard my heart against false definitions of identity and help me live boldly in the purpose you created for me. Amen.

I walk by faith and not by sight, trusting God's perfect plan for my life.

Scripture: *"For we walk by faith, not by sight." – 2 Corinthians 5:7 (NKJV)*

Devotional Reflection:

The shadow of *war* fills headlines, stirring fear and uncertainty. Yet, scripture reminds us that what we see does not define reality, faith does. While nations rage and kingdoms rise against one another, believers are called to walk in confidence, trusting God's unseen hand. Wars remind us that this world is temporary, but God's promises are everlasting. Our faith, lived out in troubled times, becomes a testimony to a watching world that hope is found not in treaties or armies but in Christ alone.

Reflection Question: Where am I allowing fear of global conflict to overshadow my trust in God's sovereignty?

____

____

____

____

____

Prayer: Lord, strengthen my faith in chaotic times. Teach me to trust your promises by peeking through the lens of your time-tested looking glass of manifested acts, which is far beyond what the world reveals. Amen.

I am strong and courageous, for the Lord my God is with me wherever I go.

Scripture: *"Have I not commanded you? Be strong and of good courage; do not be afraid, nor be dismayed, for the Lord your God is with you wherever you go." – Joshua 1:9 (NKJV)*

Devotional Reflection:

Global economic instability weighs heavily on hearts; jobs lost, inflation rising, and systems faltering. Fear whispers that survival depends on wealth or security, yet God commands His people to live with courage rooted in His presence. True strength does not come from stable markets but from the Spirit who never leaves us. Even when resources shake, God remains unshaken. Courage in these times means trusting that provision, peace, and purpose come from him alone.

Reflection Question: How can I surrender fear of financial instability and embrace God's promise to be with me always?

____

____

____

____

____

Prayer: Lord, make me courageous in times of uncertainty. Help me rest in your faithful provision instead of fearing lack. Amen.

I am more than a conqueror through Christ who loves me.

Scripture: *"Yet in all these things we are more than conquerors through Him who loved us." – Romans 8:37 (NKJV)*

Devotional Reflection:

As darkness increases, the Church must stand united. We were not designed to walk this journey alone. Being "*more than conquerors*" means not only victory in Christ individually but strength as the body of believers collectively. Together we encourage, intercede, and testify. Isolation weakens, but unity strengthens. In a time when persecution and moral decline intensify, the invitation is clear: the Church must rise as one body, conquering not through power or numbers but through Christ's love and victory on the cross.

Reflection Question: How can I strengthen the body of Christ by encouraging and uniting with other believers?

____

____

____

____

____

Prayer: Jesus, thank you for making us more than conquerors. Help me build up your body and live in unity with fellow believers. Amen.

I have peace that surpasses all understanding, guarding my heart and mind in Christ Jesus.

Scripture: *"And the peace of God, which surpasses all understanding, will guard your hearts and minds through Christ Jesus." – Philippians 4:7 (NKJV)*

Devotional Reflection:

In an age of unrest, believers are called to declare steadfastness in Christ. God's *peace* is not passive. It guards, shields, and sustains. While the world is tossed by fear and confusion, the believer can stand firm, anchored in a peace that cannot be explained by human reason. Declaring peace is declaring trust in the "One" who rules above every storm. Steadfastness is both testimony and weapon. It proclaims that we are unshaken because Christ reigns.

Reflection Question: What declarations of peace and steadfastness can I make today to strengthen my faith?

____

____

____

____

____

Prayer: Father, help me stand firm in your peace. May my steadfastness be a light in a restless world. Amen.

I am equipped and empowered to fulfill every good work God has prepared for me.

Scripture: *"For we are His workmanship, created in Christ Jesus for good works, which God prepared beforehand that we should walk in them." – Ephesians 2:10 (NKJV)*

Devotional Reflection:

To be *empowered to endure* is to live prepared; equipped by the Spirit for every challenge and every opportunity. God has not left His people defenseless. He has armed us with His Word, His Spirit, and His promises. Endurance is more than survival. It is active obedience, continuing in faith, love, and service as we await Christ's return. The world may grow darker, but the empowered believer grows brighter. To endure is to remain steadfast until the end, knowing our eternal reward is secure in Him.

Reflection Question: What steps can I take to actively endure and remain faithful as I await Christ's return?

____

____

____

____

____

Prayer: Lord, thank you for empowering me to endure. Strengthen me to finish well and be faithful until you come. Amen.

Beloved, the affirmations you have declared are not just positive words, they are prophetic truths rooted in God's eternal Word. In a world shaking with uncertainty, wars, rising fears, and rapid change, God is calling His people to stand firm, walk in empowerment, and prepare for the soon return of Christ. These affirmations are a daily reminder that your life is anchored not in the instability of culture, government, or technology but in the unshakable Kingdom of God.

Dr. Radiance L. Rose

HER EXCELLENCY, AMBASSADOR, DR. RADIANCE L. ROSE

Her Excellency, Dr. Radiance L. Rose is a modern-day renaissance woman, professionally known as an award-winning Certified Professional Life & Leadership Coach, Educator, Transformational Speaker, 5X #1 Best-Selling Author, Executive Producer & Host of Seize the Day with Coach Rai, Master Resilience Trainer, Human Rights Advocate, and Entrepreneur.

In her current role, she serves as an Aerospace Science Instructor and mentor in the Atlanta Metropolitan Area, GA. As a coach, she specializes in trauma, resilience, leadership, and human trafficking. Dr. Rose has helped thousands of people transform their lives through education, coaching, and mentorship. As the visionary founder of the X-Clusive Retreats Experience, Dr. Rose pioneers a sanctuary for multicultural women, promoting mental and emotional wellness through introspection, self-care, and holistic education. Additionally, she is the founder and director of the Ladies First Mentorship Program (LFMP), which empowers high school teens and young women to become confident leaders through education, mentorship, practical experiences/activities in self-esteem and self-care, business, leadership, etiquette, and community service.

Dr. Rose's comprehensive and versatile experience includes a record of successfully overseeing various large-scale programs and projects in the logistics and education industries. She also has extensive expertise in business management consultation, team building, professional development implementation, and corporate collaboration. Dr. Rose specializes in leadership and character development at various levels of management, with a focus on empowerment and diversity, equity, and inclusion initiatives.

Moreover, Dr. Rose is a retired combat veteran of the U.S. Air Force, where she served honorably for 22 years. She has a stellar record of philanthropy and community service, volunteering over 10,000 hours to 330 organizations. These organizations include the Global Goodwill Ambassador Foundation, the Fisher House, American Legion, Give an Hour (which focuses on veterans' mental health), American Cancer Society, American Red Cross, and March of Dimes (which focuses on eradicating preventable maternal health risks and deaths and closing the health equity gap).

Dr. Rose earned a Doctorate in Philosophy of Entrepreneurship and Business Administration along with the prestigious United Nations Global Woman of Distinction Award.

She also completed a faith-based seminary program and earned Doctorates in Divinity & Metaphysics. Furthermore, Dr. Rose earned a Master of Education in Student Affairs in Higher Education, Bachelor's Degree in Homeland Security with a Concentration in Counterterrorism Studies and Immigration Law, an Associate in Applied Science in Business & Logistics (a dual degree), an Associate of Applied Science in Instructor of Technology and Military Science, Certificates in Leadership (John Maxwell Team), Certified Life Coaching Credential (CPC), Master Resilience Trainer (MRT) Six Sigma, Diversity, Equity, & Inclusion (DEI), Myers-Briggs Type Indicator (MBTI), Four Lenses, Trauma-Informed Coaching & Counseling (TICC), and a Certificate in Resilience from Harvard University Business School.

Her professional affiliations/memberships include: Sigma Gamma Rho Sorority, Inc. (Lambda Sigma Sigma Co-Chair, Awards & Achievement Committee, SWIM 1922 & Membership Committee Member), Alpha Delta Omega Military Sorority, Inc. (former National Vice-President & Public Affairs Officer), Pi Lambda Theta Honor Society, Kappa Delta Pi, International Honor Society, Golden Key International Honour Society, National Association of Student Personnel Administrators (Conference Committee Chair, 2022), Order of the Sword & Shield National Honor Society, the Society for Collegiate Leadership & Achievement, National Council of Negro Women, National Association of Black Military Women (Metro-Atlanta Chapter), & American Legion Member.

Dr. Rose is also the recipient of the 46th President Joseph Biden Lifetime Achievement Award, 2022, and the Official Barack Obama 44th Presidential Legacy Lifetime Achievement Award, 2023.

Additionally, in March 2023, Her Excellency, Dr. Rose was appointed as a United Nations Ambassador-at-Large (New York). Her works have been featured in Times Square, Manhattan, New York and published in various magazines and articles.

As an advocate for humanity, Dr. Rose is certified in human trafficking and she regularly supports the Polaris Project, a nonprofit nongovernmental organization that works to eradicate and prevent sex and labor trafficking.

She also supports the Black and Missing Foundation, Inc., a non-profit organization whose mission is to bring awareness to missing persons of color; provide vital resources and tools to missing persons' families and friends, and to educate the minority community on personal safety.

Furthermore, Dr. Rose actively engages in community service in partnership with The Hendricks Hope Foundation, a reputable non-profit organization committed to enhancing opportunities and empowering children in foster care and at-risk communities. As a catalyst for global change, ViVi Cole Coaching & Consulting has generously contributed numerous personal hygiene kits to promote feminine health and wellness among young girls in Kenya, Africa. Dr. Rose extends her support through monthly sponsorship of young girls in Africa via the Hendricks Hope Foundation, providing financial assistance for their education and growth Prospects.

Additionally, Dr. Rose contributes to BeLoved Atlanta, a non-profit organization that has been helping women escape the sex industry in Georgia since 2012.

BeLoved Atlanta provides safe homes and a two-year restoration program rooted in both the Christian faith and proven therapeutic strategies.

For more than 20 years, Dr. Rose has helped thousands of people transform their lives and achieve their personal and professional goals through coaching and mentorship.

Driven by her powerful philosophy, Unpack it & Attack it, Dr. Rose remains an enduring source of inspiration for all the communities she passionately serves.

Let's Connect:

Her Excellency Ambassador, Radiance L. Rose, CPC, M.Ed., D.Div., Ph.D.

United Nations Ambassador

U.S. Air Force Retired Combat Veteran

President/SHE-EO, & Founder, ViVi Cole Coaching & Consulting

President & Founder, ViVi Cole Global Inc. a 501(c)(3) Organization

Brand Architect, The X-Clusive Retreat Experience

Founder & Director, Ladies First Mentorship Program

Email: rr@vivicole.com

Instagram: @therealcoachrai

Vision & Activation
Seeing Clearly and Moving Forward

Once your foundation is secure and your heart is renewed, it is time to **move**.

This section activates faith through vision, clarity, and obedience. These affirmations encourage you to trust what God has shown you, speak life over it, and take intentional steps toward what He has placed in your hands.

Manifest Your Vision

Affirmations by Apostle Dr. Deleshia Jemison

Affirmation: God has given you permission to own your position. Allow nothing to stop you.

The Word of God has given you authority to walk boldly in your assignment. Open your mouth and affirm your vision. Affirm your vision with unwavering confidence. Begin today by clearly defining your goals and values, anchoring your purpose in something meaningful. Visualize your assignment daily, using that mental image to guide decisions and actions. God has given you divine permission to own your position. Walk boldly in the authority He's placed upon your life. You are chosen, equipped, and anointed for this moment. No obstacle, opinion, or opposition can cancel what heaven has ordained. Rise with confidence, knowing you are not here by accident. Refuse to look back. The doors God opens no man can shut. Stand firm in your identity, your calling, and your voice. You have Kingdom influence. Let faith silence fear. Allow nothing to stop you. This is your time to move forward, fully aligned with divine purpose.

1Cor. 15:58 KJV says, Therefore, my beloved brethren, be ye steadfast, unmovable, always abounding in the work of the Lord, for ye know that your labor is not in vain in the Lord.

Affirmation: Where you are right now is not as important as where you are going. Your destiny Awaits You!

Circumstances may arise, but God has given you peace through His Word to understand: a *greater purpose* is ahead of you. Every day, aim towards your purpose. Embrace forward momentum. Dream bigger, take steps, stay focused and allow your destiny to push you forward. Remember that it is not where you come from, or not even where you are; it is where you are going that matters most. There is a greater purpose ahead of you. What's behind you cannot compare to what God has prepared. Keep moving forward in faith. Your trials are shaping you; your obedience is unlocking doors. Destiny awaits. Stay aligned. Stay ready. Your next chapter carries power, impact, and divine fulfillment. Your destiny awaits you!

Jeremiah 29:11KJV says, For I know the thoughts that I think toward you, saith the LORD, thoughts of peace, and not of evil, to give you an expected end.

Affirmation: Step in doors of favor. Focus on your vision. There are souls destined to meet you. You shall turn hearts in the Kingdom of God.

God is promoting you in this season. Don't be afraid to step out of your comfort zone. Step through open doors of favor that God has ordained for you—doors no one can shut, ushering in breakthroughs and divine alignment. Keep your eyes fixed on your vision; let His Word illuminate your path, guiding each confident step. Remember souls are destined to align with your journey. Know that God's timing and spiritual appointments are perfect. You will turn hearts toward the Kingdom of God, reflecting His love and favor in every encounter. Embrace this season of destiny with faith, boldness, and expectation. Your destiny awaits, shining brightly in His glory.

Isaiah 58:11 KJV says, And the LORD shall guide thee continually, and satisfy thy soul in drought, and make fat thy bones: and thou shalt be like a watered garden, and like a spring of water, whose waters fail not.

Affirmation: You are a Champion. Arise in the midst of adversity.

God's Word shall empower you today. God will not fail you nor forsake you. You shall be courageous in pursuing your assignment. Arise in this season, to conquer your enemy. Today, you shall move forward not on impulse but in clear, precise vision. You have spiritual direction. Trust in divine wisdom and the power of obedience to secure complete restoration.

1 Samuel 30:8 (KJV) says, And David enquired at the LORD, saying, Shall I pursue after this troop? shall I overtake them? And he answered him, Pursue: for thou shalt surely overtake them, and without fail recover all. You don't have to be afraid of your current circumstance. God has given you the privilege to seek him for guidance. David's question, "Shall I pursue … and overtake them?" empowers you to be determined and dependent on God. Be confident by God's promises: "Thou shalt surely overtake them, and without fail recover all." Your faith meets your assurance. Your God is with you.

Affirmation: Your vision of endurance shall give you great victory. Don't give up.

Today, God has given you *Clear Vision.* Don't allow your vision to be obscured. You are a warrior. You have the power of clear focus. A clear spiritual gateway is sufficient to conquer every battle. God has given you the victory to overcome every obstacle. Continue to hold on to the vision without wavering. Don't waiver the vision. What God placed in your heart is divine. Stay focused, even when the path seems unclear. Distractions will come, but purpose demands perseverance. Trust the process, keep believing, and walk by faith. Your vision will manifest in due time. Continue to press forward with boldness and unwavering confidence. God is with you.

Deu. 20:4 KJV says, For the LORD your God is the one who goes with you to fight for you against your enemies to give you victory.

Affirmation: You are favored by God. The enemy can't stop you.

The Favor of God has given you divine access to unlock doors in this season. This affirmation shall empower you to walk boldly in your divine identity. It's never what it appears to be. Be empowered to walk by faith. God's favor is constant. Never failing you. You are richly favored by God. You are chosen, uplifted, destined for breakthrough. God's Divine favor has shielded you, guiding your steps and opening doors no one can shut. Even in the hardest seasons, you stand anchored by grace. Your joy is complete in Jesus. His favor is constant and unshakeable. His word firmly establishes you. Walk in His divine favor. Allow it to flow from God's unmerited Grace.

Rom. 8:31 KJV says, What shall we then say to these things? If God be for us, who can be against us?

Affirmation: You are Relevant! Keep Going! God has a plan for your life!

The Bible teaches that God's plan will never disappoint us. Walk courageously and boldly into your divine destiny. You don't need validation from people. Do whatever God has called for you to do. The Word of God has given you a divine charge, teaching us the importance of courage and strength in God's presence. Trust in God's power and guidance when facing challenging situations. You are relevant. Your life has meaning and your presence carries impact. God created you with intentionality, gifting you with purpose. Your voice matters, your story matters, and your journey is not in vain. You were born for such a time as this. Don't doubt your divine significance in this world.

In Joshua 1:9, the KJV reads, Have not I commanded thee? Be strong and of good courage; be not afraid, neither be thou dismayed: for the Lord thy God is with thee whithersoever thou goest.

Dr. Deleshia Jemison

Dr. Deleshia Jemison is the founder of W.W.I.P. Women Win in Prayer Global. Deleshia received her Honorary Doctorate of Divinity from New York Christian Bible College. She is a #1 best-selling international author, forerunner, intercessor, mentor, and counselor. Deleshia currently hosts conferences to educate, equip, and empower others to know their true identity in the Kingdom of God. She also travels abroad to speak at conferences and revivals in different cities, states, and nations. Some of her prayer conference titles include: *Intercessors Realm of Authority, The Call of the Intercessor, Fire on the Altar, and Governing Authority of Prayer*. She believes in the power of intimate prayer and the Word of Truth. Deleshia believes prayer is the foundation to build, birth, and establish every ministry.

Dr. Deleshia has been anointed and equipped to enter the Apostolic, Prophetic, and Deliverance Ministry. She states that the Holy Spirit has revealed in these last days that the Body of Christ should have prayer deliverance chambers where people are delivered, healed, and set free. She is a seasoned Prophet to the Nations and has humbled herself to understand the importance of servanthood in the Kingdom of God.

Dr. Deleshia ministers to the needs of those who are broken, hurting, abused, and neglected. She has over 24 years of experience in ministry, which includes ministering to victims of human trafficking, domestic violence, and homelessness. She has also ministered to displaced youth, the elderly, abused women, and children. Dr. Deleshia's passion is winning lost souls as she walks boldly as an Ambassador of Jesus Christ.

Contact Info:

WWW.WWIPMINISTRIES.ORG

wwipministries@yahoo.com

904-516-8604

Dr. Deleshia's Acknowledgments

I thank my Lord and Savior Jesus Christ for the power of His deliverance upon my life to allow me to be His vessel in this season. Thank you Dr. Kishma George for allowing me to be a part of this collaboration. I celebrate all the authors. Keep allowing God to minister through your pen. You are changing the world. To all the hurting people, don't give up. Better days are ahead of you.

Affirmations for Daily Victory

Affirmations by Prophetess Kimberly Dillard

Affirmation: I am equipped, anointed, and unstoppable because God is with me.

"The Spirit of the Lord is upon me, because He has anointed me to proclaim good news to the poor. He has sent me to proclaim freedom for the prisoners and recovery of sight for the blind, to set the oppressed free," — Luke 4:18 (NIV)

Every good and perfect gift comes from the Lord and He has already equipped you with the wisdom, gifts and resources you need for your journey (Hebrews 13:21). Just as Jesus declared in Luke 4:18, you are anointed, which means you are chosen and empowered by the Holy Spirit—God's power rests on you to bring light, healing, and hope to the world. Understand that being unstoppable doesn't mean you won't face obstacles or challenges, but it does mean that the challenges and obstacles you face will not overtake you and they certainly cannot override God's plan for you (Romans 8:31). God's presence makes you unstoppable! Declare this affirmation boldly knowing that your identity and authority is in Christ Jesus!

Affirmation: I walk in favor, wisdom, and divine strategy.

"For the Lord gives wisdom; from his mouth come knowledge and understanding." –Proverbs 2:6 NIV

"Surely, Lord, you bless the righteous; you surround them with your favor as with a shield." –Psalm 5:12 NIV

To walk in **favor** is to carry God's blessing and approval everywhere that you go. As His favor rests upon you, you can expect open doors, opportunities, sudden surprises and even challenges to work for your good. God's favor is potent, powerful and undeniable.

Walking in Godly **wisdom i**s to reach beyond human reasoning and instead make choices that are influenced by His insight and understanding. Wisdom is readily available to every believer and God will give it generously when you ask without wavering. God never leaves us to figure out life alone. He will give you **divine strategy**, which includes specific timing and direction for every season in your life. He equips you for every circumstance providing the exact steps you must take for breakthrough and success. With God's guidance you can be assured that even when the path isn't clear His wisdom lights your way, His favor shields you and His strategies position you for victory. Declare this affirmation daily and align your thoughts and actions with the reality of God's Kingdom!

Affirmation: I am grateful for growth, wisdom, and divine protection.

"But grow in the grace and knowledge of our Lord and Savior Jesus Christ. To him be glory both now and forever!" –2 Peter 3:18 (NIV)

"For he will command his angels concerning you to guard you in all your ways." –Psalm 91:11 (NIV)

Every lesson you've learned and every season endured has prepared you for a greater purpose. This affirmation is a reminder to see the hand of the Lord in every part of your journey. Expressing gratitude for **growth** is an indicator that you recognize that even the challenges have shaped and strengthened you (2 Peter 3:18).

Being thankful for **wisdom** is an acknowledgement of God's gift of insight and understanding in your life. God's **divine protection** is something we need every second of the day, so praise Him for it. Psalm 91:11 tells us that He commands His angels to guard you in all your ways. Even when you can't see, God is shielding you from harm, surrounding you with His care. Say this affirmation with a heart of thankfulness and be confident that God is protecting you, growing you and pouring out His wisdom upon you.

Affirmation: I am victorious and I triumph over every challenge!

"But thanks be to God! He gives us the victory through our Lord Jesus Christ." –1 Corinthians 15:57 (NIV)

Faith and resilience is your portion and through God's power every obstacle becomes an opportunity for His glory to shine through you. Remember that your **triumph** isn't reliant on your ability but on Jesus who has already overcome the world. Releasing this affirmation daily will build your confidence in the promises of God and keep you anchored in **victory**.

Affirmation: I am a trailblazer anointed to break barriers and pioneer new paths.

"See, I am doing a new thing! Now it springs up; do you not perceive it?" –Isaiah 43:19

"The Spirit of the Sovereign Lord is on me, because the Lord has anointed me to proclaim good news to the poor. He has sent me to bind up the brokenhearted, to proclaim freedom for the captives and release from darkness for the prisoners." –Isaiah 61:1

Declaring this affirmation daily affirms that you are uniquely chosen to go places where others have never gone. Trailblazers carry courage, vision and innovation to establish new standards, open new doors and create opportunities for others. By His Spirit the Lord will equip you to do what seems impossible including breaking barriers. To break barriers is about overcoming limitations that have held others back. Those barriers can be cultural, spiritual, personal or professional, but regardless God will empower you to dismantle them and pioneer new paths into new territories. When you walk as a trailblazer and create paths for others to walk on, you inspire others to dream bigger, press forward and answer the call on their life.

Speak this affirmation to remind yourself that your journey is not just about you but there are others waiting for you to blaze the trail, light the path and lead them to greater. Your journey is not ordinary—God created you to create change and leave a legacy that others will follow.

Prophetess Kimberly Dillard

Kimberly Dillard is a yielded vessel to God, a prophetic writer, mentor, inspirational speaker, life coach, businesswoman and television show host whose life reflects her deep commitment to faith, purpose, and people. With a passion for prayer and a heart for transformation, she has devoted her life to helping others recognize their God-given calling and walk boldly into destiny.

As a prophetic voice, Kimberly brings encouragement, wisdom, and revelation to those she mentors and leads. Her words carry the weight of authenticity, birthed from her own seasons of pressing, healing, and perseverance. At the center of her life and work are her core values: love, family, salvation, healing, deliverance, and intercession. Kimberly is the CEO of Arise Inspiration LLC and the president of Love Ambassadors for Christ Ministry.

Connect with Kimberly at-

Email: dillardkimberly@outlook.com

Website: kimberlydillard.com

IG: iamkimberlydillard

FB: Kimberly Dillard

YT: The Prophetic Hope w/Kimberly Dillard

The Fulfilled Life

Affirmations by Kesha Robinson

I am walking in the overflow of blessings, abundance and uncommon favor.

The Bible declares, according to James 1:17 (NIV), "Every good and perfect gift is from above, coming down from the Father of the heavenly lights, who does not change like shifting shadows." It also states that "God is able to bless you abundantly, so that in all things at all times, having all that you need, you will abound in every good work" according to 2 Corinthians 9:8 (NIV). With God on our side, we have supernatural provision and favor. Favor is not earned; it is freely given through faith in Christ. God's favor is a gift that is given to us because of His grace and love. Scripture offers this encouragement, "…for the Lord your God is bringing you into a good land—a land with brooks, streams, and deep springs gushing out into the valleys and hills…" (Deuteronomy 8:7 NIV)

Declare: "Blessings and favor follow me everywhere I go."

I have what it takes to win and fulfill my dreams and purpose.

Habakkuk 2:2–3 (NKJV) advises us to document our God-given vision. "Write the vision and make *it* plain on tablets, that he may run who reads it. For the vision *is* yet for an appointed time." The Bible instructs in Proverbs 16:3 (NIV), "Commit to the Lord whatever you do, and he will establish your plans." You have a bright future ahead. " For I know the plans I have for you," declares the LORD, "plans to prosper you and not to harm you, plans to give you hope and a future." (Jeremiah 29:11 NIV)

Declare: "I have a fulfilling life and the best is yet to come."

I am loved, chosen, made new, enough, victorious, forgiven, and never alone.

Scripture teaches us that believers are chosen by God for a special purpose. This was a choice He made before the foundation of the world. God also assures us through His Word, "My grace is sufficient for you, for my power is made perfect in weakness." (2 Corinthians 12:9 NIV) This is very encouraging because it lets us know that our weaknesses do not make us inadequate but provides an opportunity for God to demonstrate His power. We are more than conquerors. God is with us. He said in His Word, "the LORD your God goes with you; he will never leave you nor forsake you." (Deuteronomy 31:6 NIV) We are also assured in 2 Corinthians 5:17 (NKJV), "Therefore, if anyone *is* in Christ, *he is* a new creation; old things have passed away; behold, all things have become new."

Declare: "I am the righteousness of God in Christ Jesus."

I am God's masterpiece—fearfully and wonderfully made.

According to Ephesians 2:10 (NIV), "For we are God's handiwork, created in Christ Jesus to do good works, which God prepared in advance for us to do." God made no mistakes when he made you. Psalm139:13–14 (NIV) makes it clear: "…for you created my inmost being; you knit me together in my mother's womb. I praise you because I am fearfully and wonderfully made; your works are wonderful, I know that full well." God is the potter and we are the clay. "Yet you, LORD, are our Father. We are the clay, you are the potter; we are all the work of your hand." (Isaiah 64:8 NIV) We are made in His likeness and in His image.

Declare: "I am a vessel of honor for God's use."

I can accomplish anything I set my mind to as God establishes my plans.

Scripture tells us in Matthew 19:26 (NIV) "…with man this is impossible, but with God all things are possible." We must believe it if we want to achieve it. "Commit your way to the Lord, Trust also in Him, And He shall bring it to pass." (Psalm 37:5 NKJV). We also have the assurance through His Word that "I can do all things through Christ who strengthens me." (Philippians 4:13)

Declare: "Everything I set my hands to will prosper."

I am a blessing to others that I encounter.

We are blessed to be a blessing. Genesis 12:2 (NKJV) says, "I will make you a great nation; I will bless you and make your name great; And you shall be a blessing.

Then, Proverbs 11:25 (NIV) states that "a generous person will prosper; whoever refreshes others will be refreshed." Jesus taught the importance of loving without conditions, being generous, and showing kindness.

Declare: "I am valuable, I am important, and I make a difference."

I walk in peace, I am surrounded by God's goodness, and I rest in God's presence.

Romans 15:13 (NIV) offers the encouragement, "May the God of hope fill you with all joy and peace as you trust in him so you may overflow with hope by the power of the Holy Spirit." Psalm 34:8 (NIV) says, "Taste and see that the Lord is good; blessed is the one who takes refuge in him." Scripture promises that, "Surely goodness and mercy shall follow me All the days of my life; And I will dwell in the house of the Lord Forever." (Psalm 23:6 NKJV)

Declare: "I walk in perfect peace because my mind is steadfast on God."

Kesha Robinson

Kesha Robinson is a best-selling author, business owner, mentor, and creative entrepreneur in the Washington, DC area. With a background in radiology, Kesha had her career path all planned out; however, God had a completely different plan for her. She is now the proud owner of Spic & Span Cleaning Company, established in 2012, and has been self-employed since then. She also serves as the executive producer for her daughter's YouTube platform, Sunshine's Toca, and television platform, Zoey TV, an educational and entertainment platform promoting positivity, creativity and literacy. Additionally, she serves as technical director for the media ministry at her church, as well as a producer and editor for various other organizations and platforms.

Kesha is the author of twelve children's books, along with her daughter Zoey, and three additional books that she authored and co-authored. The children's books are designed to empower children in the areas of self-esteem, integrity, leadership, acts of kindness and more.

Kesha and Zoey both have been featured nationally in magazines, on radio shows, podcasts, the news, and other media outlets throughout the years. Kesha is passionate about helping individuals fulfill their God-given purpose as well as offering job opportunities for others. She is a natural encourager and loves to see people win! Kesha plans to continue running her cleaning company, publishing books and producing content that will inspire audiences around the world.

Kesha's Acknowledgements

I would like to thank God for this incredible opportunity and for guiding my life and for every open door He has granted me access to. I am ever so grateful, Lord, for the life you prepared and planned for me before I was formed in my mother's womb.

I'd like to acknowledge my leaders, **Apostle Wayne & Prophetess Michelle Green**, for being so phenomenal, consistent and loving throughout the years. I am happy that God saw fit to send me to your ministry. It has changed my life forever.

Also to my **church family**, I love you all. Thank you for the kindness, love and amazing memories and more to come.

To my beautiful and amazing **mom**. You taught me so much about being a great mom because you are one. You raised us to be God-fearing and we are. You raised us to have a solid and strong education and we do. You are truly a jewel and I am so grateful to be blessed with a mom like you. I wouldn't trade it for anything.

To my **dad**, my amazing, loving and wonderful dad. You are my friend, my example, my laughing partner, my storyteller, my listening ear. You are such a phenomenal father and I'm so blessed to have you in my life.

To my **brother**, words can't even describe you accurately. You are the absolute best brother I could ever have asked for or dreamed of. You have such a kind heart, a loving spirit and you are HILARIOUS! The funniest person I know. You keep shining. I can't wait for all of your dreams to come true. You deserve the absolute best and I pray that you receive everything your heart desires.

To my beautiful, amazing and talented daughter **Zoey**, my love for you is endless. You make me so proud to be a mom. From the moment I first laid eyes on you, I was in love. From the first time I felt you move in my tummy, I was in love. From the first day you came home from the hospital, I was in love. You make parenting easy. You are easy to love; you are obedient and such a sweet, kind and loving child. I am more than blessed to have you for my daughter. I thank God for you every day.

To my mentor, **Dr. Kishma George**, I have so much love and appreciation for you. You are such a jewel. I am forever grateful for all you have done for us and for all of the many incredible opportunities throughout the years. Most importantly, thank you for believing in me, pushing me, and always keeping it real with me. I would not be where I am today had God not placed you in my life. You are the epitome of GRACE, EXCELLENCE, STYLE, CLASS, WISDOM, and BEAUTY. I am inspired by you daily. You are truly and completely walking in purpose and changing lives throughout the world. Your methods are unmatched and I'm so thankful to have you in my life and in my daughter's life as a mentor and friend.

To **Dr. Denise Wade**, where do I start other than to tell you that you mean the world to me? You show me every day what true friendship is really about. You are one of the most consistent and wise people I know. You've been there for the highs and lows. I truly value you. You are amazing, beautiful, loving and indeed one of a kind. You have been such a phenomenal friend over the years.

You are irreplaceable. I love you so much and I couldn't ask God for a better friend.

To **Dana, Tamika, Stephanie, Tiffany, Erica, LaShelle, Mikey, Chris, Courtney, Tai, Ashley, Neicey**, and all of my other friends. I appreciate and love you more than you know.

To **my aunts, uncles, cousins, extended family, godparents Aunt Jackie and Uncle Richard, Mia, Ethan and my entire family**, I LOVE YOU ALL SO MUCH!

My God Is a Promise Keeper Who Will Never Leave Me Nor Forsake Me

Affirmations by Dr. Delsue Frankson

Affirmation Statements and Explanations

I am safe, guided and protected daily.

I am so grateful that because I am a child of God, I do not have to live in fear. The Word of God reminds us that "He that dwelleth in the secret place of the Most High Shall rest in the shadow of the Almighty." Psalm 91:1 (NIV) Begin each day with confidence, knowing that God is watching over you.

I am blessed because the Lord provides the desires of my heart.

I am so grateful for the promises of God. Psalm 37:4 (NIV) reminds us that "If we take delight in the Lord, He will give us the desires of our hearts." Rest in the promises of God and watch the desires of your heart come to past.

I am filled with joy.

I am so grateful for the gift of joy that is given to us as children of God. The Word of God reminds us that "the joy of the Lord is our strength." Nehemiah 8:10 (NIV) This verse reminds us to enjoy each day that the Lord has given us. Share the Gospel and our blessings with each other. Find the joy in each day because the Lord has made a way both through salvation and our daily provisions.

I am at peace and content.

I am at peace and content because the Word reminds me in Isaiah 26:3 (NIV) that "He will keep me in perfect peace because my mind is stayed on Him." Focus on the things of God daily and you will be at peace and content on your journey through life.

I am equipped with the knowledge needed to fulfill my purpose.

I am so grateful that God has given me access to wisdom and knowledge that has equipped me for my purpose. The Word of God says that "we must ask for wisdom and the Lord will give it to us to know Him better." Ephesians 1:17 (NIV) I am so excited that we have a God that is ever present and who delights in sharing His divine wisdom and knowledge with his children who seek Him.

I am a productive and responsible global citizen.

I am so grateful for the example of the Proverbs 31 Woman in the Bible. Her example has taught me the importance of being a responsible and productive woman of God. Allow the Lord to develop the gifts He has placed in you. Your gifts will make room for you on your journey through life as you meet the needs of others.

I have everything that I need to sustain me on my journey through life.

I am so grateful for the blessings that I have received on my journey because I am a child of God. Psalm 23:6 (NIV) reminds us that "surely goodness and mercy shall follow us all the days of our lives." Contiue to trust the Lord and He will continue to provide your needs on your journey through life.

Dr. Delsue Frankson

Dr. Delsue Frankson was born in St. Elizabeth, Jamaica, West Indies and has been residing in Florida now for over 34 years. She is a minister, a life coach, a mental health coach, an educational consultant, an artist, a musician, and a fashion designer. She fell in love with working in the ministry as a little girl while assisting her mother in making offering envelopes for the Beersheba Moravian Church in their community in St. Elizabeth. She also became passionate about music after accompanying her mother who sang in the church choir to her rehearsals. After moving to the United States, her family joined the Deerfield Beach Church of God of Prophecy Ministry for over 19 years. Whilst there, she served as a member of the "New Faith" five-part harmony girls' singing group, as a youth pastor, choir director, and as a member of the praise and worship team. She also previously ministered with the South Florida Church of God of Prophecy District 2 "One Voice" choir and the "Tri-County Praise Project" choir. She also ministered with the Florida Sunshine Brass Band for over seven years locally, nationally, and throughout the Caribbean. She is currently a minister at St. John Missionary Baptist Church in Boynton Beach, Florida, where she currently serves on the pulpit ministry team in various capacities.

She has been a professional educator now for over 23 years and currently works as a behavioral and mental health instructional specialist for the school district of Palm Beach County. She is a graduate of Florida Atlantic University where she received a Bachelor's Degree in Varying Exceptionalities in 2001 and a Master's Degree in Mental Retardation in 2003. She was the recipient of the I.M.P.A.C. Award for Individuals Making Personal Academic Achievements and Giving Back to their Community from Florida Atlantic University in 2001. Her colleagues nominated her twice for the prestigious Dwyer Award for outstanding educators in Palm Beach County. She participated in several university guest lectures at Florida International University on "Classification Issues & Placement Issues and Overrepresentation" of minorities in special education. She also presented at several professional national conferences on urban special education issues. She is a published researcher and two-time Amazon best-selling author.

She was featured in the *K.I.S.H. Magazine* November 2019 issue and December 2019 issue as one of the Top 30 Most Influential Women: Movers & Shakers and *K.I.S.H. Magazine* spring edition in March 2021 as one of the Top 24 Trailblazers on the Move and *K.I.S.H. Magazine* winter 2024 "Top 15 Women to Watch and Top 13 Influential Authors to Know in 2024. She was a cast member of a new television series in the fall of 2021, *The Dreamer in You Show*, on Dominion. TV. She is the CEO of Delsue Frankson Consulting Services LLC and Perseverance University. She launched a music therapy project for children, "Good Night", in 2021. She is a model and fashion designer and her shoe brand Grit was featured in Italy, the United Kingdom, the United States of America, and *Asia and Elle* magazine in November 2020.

She was initiated into the Xi Pi Omega Chapter of Alpha Kappa Alpha Sorority Incorporated in the fall of 2012 as a part of "The Ten Cultured Pearls." She is a "Top Mentor" on the new "Wisdom App". She was recently selected to be a conference proposal reviewer for the national 2024 Mental Health First Aid Summit in St. Louis, Missouri and was invited to participate in the international "Rebuilding Ukraine" Forum in Romania in October 2023. She recently graduated on October 18, 2023 with an Education Specialist Degree in Organizational Leadership from Grand Canyon University and is currently completing her doctoral degree capstone "Strategic Research Project" in Organizational Leadership at Nova Southeastern University. She also received an Honorary Doctorate in Divinity from the School of the Great Commission Theological Seminary in West Columbia, South Carolina on December 16, 2023. She desires to complete her doctoral degree and continue to make a significant difference in the field of education, in her community, and in the world. She brings her passion for service and for helping people to succeed and her experience as a leader and a team player to the field of education and the world. She hopes to continue to be a change agent and to help others become productive and responsible global citizens.

Contact Information (website, social media name, etc.)

Website: https://linktr.ee/DelsueFranksonConsulting

Instagram: @delsue_frankson

Instagram: @grit_italianfashion

Personal Facebook: https://www.facebook.com/delsue.frankson/

Business Facebook

Page: https://www.facebook.com/DelsueFranksonConsulting

LinkedIn: https://www.linkedin.com/in/DelsueFrankson/

Delsue's Acknowledgments

My contribution to this affirmation book project is dedicated to everyone who entered my life and made a difference. All glory, praise and honor belong to God for giving me the wisdom and knowledge needed to contribute to this project. Special thanks to my parents Basil and Doreen Frankson for being the best parents to a strong-willed little girl who now has matured into a woman who is led by God. Thank you both for supporting my dreams and for allowing me to spread my wings and fly. To my siblings and first friends, thank you for recognizing the calling on my life and for being my cheerleaders. To my amazing nieces and nephews, thank you for your continuous words of encouragement. Special thanks to all my so-called "Frankson Kids" who crossed my path as an educator. Thank you all for allowing me to make a difference in your lives, which helped me develop the skillsets that I have today. My contribution is designed to help individuals become successful in fulfilling their dreams and purpose in life. My goal is to encourage individuals to persevere regardless of the obstacles that they will face in life. Walk in your destiny!

Purpose & Authority

Walking in What You Carry

Purpose is not accidental, and authority is not earned—it is assigned.

This section strengthens your confidence to walk fully in your God-given assignment. These affirmations affirm leadership, responsibility, and spiritual authority, empowering you to stand firm, lead well, and steward what God has entrusted to you.

Beautifully Scarred

Affirmations by Evangelist-Dr. Wanda S. Briscoe

Affirmation: I am beautiful with my scars and nothing is wrong with me.

The Bible teaches us that even if you have scars, you are beautiful and you should not think that something is wrong with you. Don't let the scars make you think that you are "less than" a person. Don't let anyone tell you that, due to your scars, you don't matter. The Bible tells us that "We are fearfully and wonderfully made." God doesn't make junk. He does all things well.

As you confess this affirmation daily, remember that you are beautiful with your scars. (Song of Solomon 4:7 NLT) Trust in the beauty of flaws and that you are marked with greatness.

Affirmation: I am designed in greatness.

The Bible tells us that we are God's masterpiece and we should never think that we are not. We should walk with our heads held high every day knowing that God designed us in His image. God molded and shaped each of us in a unique way. Our uniqueness is what makes us amazing. Embrace who you are because you can't be duplicated!

As you confess this affirmation daily, smile and lift your head up knowing that you are God's masterpiece (Ephesians 2:10 NLT)

Affirmation: I am rare and valuable.

The Bible refers to this type of woman as someone whose godly traits are rare and valuable. We are royalty and we should stand firm in this. We are worthy and God calls us His friend. Isn't it amazing how He created us and no two people are the same? We are rare, unique, valuable, royal, and extraordinary!

As you confess this affirmation daily, let it encourage you that you are worthy, one of a kind and precious. (Proverb 31:10 NLT b-clause)

Affirmation: I am healed and God has closed my wounds.

The physical scars may be on your body, but God has made you whole. Scars are beautiful! If you have scars like I have due to breast cancer, you should have the confidence in knowing that God has closed your wounds and you are healed, whole and beautiful. I recite Nahum 1:9 every day and this is my assurance that I am healed.

As you confess this affirmation daily, thank and praise God for making you whole. Your wounds are closed and the past is forgotten. (Jeremiah 30:17 NLT)

Affirmation: I am beautifully scarred and I wear my scars as a badge of honor.

If you have external scars, wear them proudly. They are a sign that you went through something and you survived. Whatever scars that you have, they made you a warrior. You are more than a conqueror! Use your scars as a testimony to encourage someone who is going through difficult times.

As you confess this affirmation daily, touch your scar or scars and say, "Father God, I am your child and I thank you for making me a warrior!" (Galatians 6:17 NLT b-clause)

Evangelist Dr. Wanda Briscoe

Wanda S. Briscoe is from St. Mary's County, Maryland, and she is the mother of three adult sons (two living and one deceased), a grandmother to three granddaughters, and a dog mom. Wanda retired from the Federal government in 2025 after serving the public for 39 years.

Literacy

To date, Wanda has written 10 books (five that she authored and five that she co-authored). The books and journals that she has authored on her own are: *The Fight Within*, *The Storm Has a Ministry Too*, *The Tears of Hannah*, *Dear Loved One*, *Things That I Want To Tell You: A 365 Grief and Loss Journal*, and *Your Yes Is Non-Negotiable*. The books that Wanda has co-authored are: *The Art of Activation*, *Mary Up: Making Art Recycling Your Used Products*, *Inspired by Love*, *The Tears of a Lonely Mother*, and *Birthing the Dreamer in You*. Wanda is a multi-best-selling author on Amazon.

Kingdom Platforms and Awards

Wanda has had the opportunity to grace the cover of three magazines, *Southern Maryland Women* (twice) and *Gospel 4 U* for her breast cancer awareness. She has received special recognition letters from former First Lady Michelle Obama for her book *The Fight Within*. On April 21, 2024, she received the Presidential Lifetime Achievement Award, in Dallas, Texas. This award is the highest honor on Earth from President Joe Biden. On April 26, 2025, at the Presidential Lifetime Achievement Award Gala in Fairfax, Virginia, she was presented with the Forerunner Award for honor and distinction and she also received the honorary Degree of Doctor of Humane Letters Honoris Causa from Bridge Builders University. On August 16, 2025, *K.I.S.H. Magazine* named Wanda as one of the Top 11 National Influencers on the Move on a billboard in New York Times Square.

Advocacy

Wanda is a member of the Sisters at Heart Breast Cancer Support Group of Southern Maryland and a member of the Pink-Bold-Beautiful breast cancer groups in Maryland. She is active in both groups and continues to offer education, inspiration, prayer, and mentorship. On December 3, 2018, her youngest son (Darryl) was murdered in Atlanta, GA at the age of 22. Due to this tragedy, she became active in the national organization Moms Demand Action for Gun Sense in America, which consists of over 10 million volunteers across the nation. Wanda uses her story to educate others on gun violence and the impact that it has in our communities.

Business

Wanda is the CEO of Healing Hearts Global Ministries (HHGM) LLC, which was founded in 2025. HHGM provides support to those facing grief, loss, trauma, and the life-altering journey of breast cancer. God has enlarged HHGM to grow into an international ministry offering counseling, advocacy, speaking engagements, and life-transforming training and workshops. Wanda is a certified grief and loss councilor by the National Association of Christian Counselors. Various churches from across the nation refer their leaders, family, and friends to Wanda for grief and loss counseling. Wanda wrote *Standard Operating Procedures in Bereavement* and she trains pastors on how to start bereavement ministries in their churches. As a certified forgiveness coach, Wanda also provides forgiveness coaching.

Media

In September 2019, Wanda debuted her weekly show on WBGR Gospel Network entitled *Wanda's Warriors Show*. In early 2023, *Wanda's Warriors Show* debuted on Zenith TV Network and the show was also on various podcast platforms (Spotify, Amazon Music, and Deezer). God opened the door for the *Wanda's Warriors Show* to be heard in Belgium, the United States, France, Russia, Nigeria, the United Kingdom, Sierra Leone, and Germany. Wanda is currently the host for the "Monday Motivation" podcast, which is a division of HHGM, and it airs on YouTube, Spotify Amazon Music, Apple podcast, iHeart Radio and all other audio streaming platforms.

Ministry

Wanda is an ordained evangelist and she is transparent with the traumas and tragedies in her life, meaning her audience relates to her compassion, authenticity, and her conquering spirit that God has instilled in her. Wanda is a sought-after global speaker, global influencer, mentor, and counselor and she loves uplifting others by sharing her stories of triumph. She has spoken in Paris, France, and London, United Kingdom. Wanda is looking forward to traveling more and spreading the Gospel of Jesus Christ around the world.

Contact information:

Website: www.healingheartsglobalministries.com

IG: hhglobalministries (business)

Email: info@healingheartsglobalministries.com

YouTube: @Wanda Briscoe TV

Wanda's Acknowledgements

First and foremost, I want to give God all the glory and honor as He has truly blessed me in ways that I never imagined. I love you, Lord, with all my heart and I thank you for restoration and for making me whole. All of the pain birthed purpose and I will forever give you praise.

In memory of my youngest son, Darryl Dennis, II, and my beloved and graceful mother, Mary A. Briscoe, I am thankful for the inspiration, the encouragement, the prayers, the calls, the texts, the videos, the hugs, and the love from the both of you. I shared so many of my dreams and things that I wanted to accomplish in life with the both of you and I am living them out. Thank you and I will forever honor the both of you and keep your memory alive.

I am thankful for my sons (Jarren and Jaquan), my daughter-in-law (Natalie), and my three granddaughters (Sage, Jaylie, and Nehlani). All of you are my special gifts of love. I'm so grateful to God for the love, joy, and laughter that you bring to my life.

I give honor to my pastors, Bishop James Polly and Prophetess Tonja Polly. Thank you for your support, your push, your encouragement, and your prayers. Thank you for seeing the God in me and pushing me further to do what God has called me to do. I love you both and I pray Deuteronomy 1:11 over your lives.

To my closest group of friends (you know who you are), thank you for your encouragement, your wise counsel, your correction, and your prayers, I love you all dearly!

Women Walking Boldly in Purpose

Affirmations by Dr. Rhonda Turner-Williams

Introduction

Every woman carries a divine assignment that cannot be duplicated. God has uniquely designed us with gifts, strengths, and testimonies that shape our purpose. Too often, women wrestle with self-doubt, comparison, or fear that blinds them from embracing the beauty of their calling. But when we root our identity in Christ, we are reminded that our worth and purpose are already established by God.

This chapter is a reminder that knowing your purpose is not about striving to be more; it's about standing firmly in who God already created you to be. As women, when we walk confidently in our purpose, we not only transform our own lives but we inspire, empower, and create a legacy for generations to follow.

Affirmation Statements & Explanations

I boldly embrace my God-given purpose as a woman of faith and strength.

Jeremiah 29:11 (NIV) assures us that God has plans to prosper us and not to harm us, plans to give us hope and a future. As women, our faith gives us the courage to rise above doubt and live with conviction. Embracing your purpose daily means choosing to walk confidently, no matter the challenges.

I am uniquely chosen by God and my purpose is valuable and needed.

Ephesians 2:10 (NIV) reminds us that we are God's workmanship, created in Christ Jesus to do good works, which God prepared in advance for us to do. Every woman has something meaningful to contribute. You are not an afterthought; you are chosen on purpose, for purpose.

I release fear and comparison and I trust God's plan for my life as a woman of purpose.

Isaiah 41:10 (KJV) declares, "Fear thou not; for I am with thee: be not dismayed; for I am thy God: I will strengthen thee; yea, I will help thee; yea, I will uphold thee with the right hand of my righteousness." Too often, women measure themselves against others, but your assignment is uniquely yours. Releasing fear and comparison makes room for faith to flourish, allowing you to walk in your own lane with joy and assurance.

I shine as a light, using my purpose to empower other women.

Matthew 5:14 (NIV) tells us, "You are the light of the world. A town built on a hill cannot be hidden." Living in purpose is never selfish—it empowers, uplifts, and encourages others. As women, we become role models when we let our light shine boldly in every season of life.

I am strengthened by God to overcome obstacles and fulfill my purpose.

Romans 8:28 (NIV) reminds us that "…in all things God works for the good of those who love him, who have been called according to his purpose." Obstacles are not meant to break you but to refine you. As a woman of purpose, you can face trials knowing that they prepare you for greater.

I live intentionally, making daily choices that honor my purpose and calling.

Proverbs 19:21 (NIV) says, "Many are the plans in a person's heart, but it is the Lord's purpose that prevails." Living intentionally means aligning your actions with God's will. Each decision you make can push you closer to the life God has designed for you.

I am a vessel of purpose, called to leave a legacy of faith for future generations of women.

Psalm 78:4 (NIV) instructs us, "We will not hide them from their descendants; we will tell the next generation the praiseworthy deeds of the Lord, his power, and the wonders he has done." Your life is a living testimony and every step you take in purpose influences the women and girls watching you. Your legacy of faith and obedience will echo for years to come.

Dr. Rhonda Williams-Turner

Dr. Rhonda Williams-Turner is a dynamic leader, author, and community advocate from Palm Beach County, Florida. She is the founder and CEO of **4 Knowledge Is Power, Inc.**, a nonprofit dedicated to strengthening families through youth development, marriage enrichment, and educational programs. Her mission is to create opportunities that empower individuals to grow, lead, and build lasting legacies.

An **11-time bestselling author**, Dr. Rhonda has published books and mini journals that inspire personal growth, faith, and relationship success. She is also the visionary behind **The Marriage Institute™, The Wife Blueprint™, and Women Business Connect™**, each providing tools and platforms for women, wives, and entrepreneurs to thrive in purpose and leadership.

With a heart for service and a passion for women's empowerment, Dr. Rhonda continues to uplift communities through her writing, coaching, and nonprofit initiatives, equipping others to lead with confidence, love, and integrity.

Dr. Rhonda's Acknowledgments

I first give all honor and glory to God, who is the author and finisher of my faith and the giver of my purpose. Without His guidance and grace these affirmations would not have been possible. I am deeply grateful to my family for their unwavering love, prayers, and encouragement. Your belief in me has strengthened my walk and reminded me daily of the importance of living in purpose.

To the women who inspire me—sisters, friends, and fellow trailblazers—thank you for walking boldly in your own callings and reminding me that we are stronger together. Your light encourages me to keep shining mine. I also acknowledge the visionaries behind this project for creating a platform where voices of faith and empowerment can come together to uplift and inspire others. It is an honor to be part of a collective work that will impact generations.

May these affirmations serve as a reminder that every woman has a God-given purpose and when we choose to live it out boldly, we not only transform our own lives but leave a legacy of faith, strength, and hope for others.

I Am Unstoppable

Affirmations by Apostle Dr. Angela Roberson

I see open doors, new God-given opportunities set before me.

When you trust in the Lord with all your heart, the Word of God directs you. You begin to see open doors, new opportunities where others do not see them. The Word of God in you removes cataracts that hinder your vision, it melts away demonic wax that hinders you from hearing God's direction towards doors meant for your elevation *"See, I have placed before you an open door that no one can shut. I know that you have little strength, yet you have kept my word."* **(Revelation 3:8 NIV)** You must see the door to be able to walk through the open door of opportunity set before you.

I am being transformed; my life reflects the glorious image of my Lord Jesus Christ.

A child of God must rest in the assurance of what is possible by the anointing irrespective of the daunting challenges, hardship, rejection and failures you might be facing in your day to day. The anointing of the Holy Spirit transforms, bringing change so you can reflect Jesus in all that you do—your speech, mannerism, how you love and care for God's people. *"So all of us who have had that veil removed can see and reflect the glory of the Lord. And the Lord—who is the Spirit—makes us more and more like him as we are changed into his glorious image."* **(2 Corinthians 3:18 NLT)**

I am highly covered and protected. I fear no evil for the Lord is with me.

Three hundred and sixty-five times the Bible tells us not to fear. Each day of your life is represented by each time the Word of God tells you not to fear. This means that God has you covered, shielded, protected from all evil. The Bible tells us not to let our hearts be troubled or let them be fearful. There is peace that comes with knowing that the Lord is with you. Rest in that knowledge and see yourself surrounded by the armies of heaven. Those with you are mightier. *"Don't be afraid, for I am with you. Don't be discouraged, for I am your God. I will strengthen you and help you. I will hold you up with my victorious right hand."* **(Isaiah 41:10 NLT)**

I am unstoppable; great and effective doors are open unto me.

When great and effective doors (doors of opportunity) are open unto you, you will meet opposition. Do not lose heart in the midst of opposition. Even with opposition looming around there are destiny helpers waiting to meet you, to help you get to your glorious destiny. It can be in academics, in business, in ministry or family. When doors of opportunity open unto you, you will find favour with men who matter; decision-makers will gravitate towards you. Hold steadfast to the promises of God for they are YES and AMEN, no matter how much they can try to oppose you. *"For a great and effective door has opened to me, and there are many adversaries."* **(1 Corinthians 16:9 NKJV)** With God you are UNSTOPPABLE.

I am fruitful. Whatever I do prospers in the mighty name of Jesus Christ.

Fruitfulness is commanded by God. In the book of Genesis, God told Adam and Eve to be fruitful. It is commanded by heaven that you bear fruit; that the works of your hands prosper. When you know this truth, you will begin to walk in the knowledge of one who hears God speak directly to them through scriptures. You will arise as one who has multiple streams of income open to them, one who recognises Jesus as the living water spoken about in the book of Revelation, and like a tree planted by the rivers of water bearing fruit in its season, your leaves will never wither. *"He shall be like a tree planted by the [a] rivers of water, That brings forth its fruit in its season, Whose leaf also shall not wither; And whatever he does shall prosper."* **(Psalm1:3)** With Jesus, prosperity is your portion.

I am victorious over every plan of the enemy in the mighty name of Jesus Christ.

Be aware and vigilant against the enemy's schemes so he does not take advantage of you. He can plant evil that lie dormant only to wait for an opportune moment to raise its head and manifest. Deadly devices of the devil are **Disappointment, Doubt, Discouragement** and **Division,** and if not nipped in the butt, they will wait for an opportunity to manifest and destabilize you. Being a believer is not a licence to be naïve or complacent. Learn to recognise things for what they are and uproot them in the name of Jesus. "*But He answered and said, 'Every plant which My heavenly Father has not planted will be uprooted.'"* **(Matthew 15:13 NKJV)**

I am given longevity of life; my life will not be cut short in the mighty name of Jesus Christ.

God has a purpose for your life, therefore your life will not be prematurely ended; your life will not be tragically cut short. Surely there is a future; that which you hope for will not be cut off. The purposes of God in your life shall be fulfilled. Knowing this will cause you to stand on the Word of God and His promises for your life, being assured of His ability to wipe away tears, stop death in its tracts, preserve you for His glory. *"And God will wipe away every tear from their eyes; there shall be no more death, nor sorrow, nor crying. There shall be no more pain, for the former things have passed away."* **(Revelations 21:4 NKJV)**

Apostle Angela Roberson

The Prophet, Apostle Angela Roberson is known as an Apostle of Prayer. She is a California native, a mother of three sons: Brian Hilt, Mark Carter and Angelo Carter.

Apostle Angela is an entrepreneur, a global speaker, the CEO and founder of Heart 2 Heart Ministries International Foundation, Heart 2 Heart Food Pantry, Heart 2 Heart Multi- Purpose Centre, and the CEO of True Kingdom Records and also the television host of *Prayer Saved My Life.*

By the grace of God, she is now the founder of her own television network "Daughter of the King TV Network." Angela has her Bachelor's degree in Biblical Studies and Counseling.

It was a push from several great leaders with Godly mentoring and counseling that led Apostle Roberson to the ministry of prayer and deliverance where she established her initial center to serve God's people. Heart 2 Heart Ministry International Foundation was birthed in Ghana, Africa, which led her to many other countries: Jamaica, Mexico, and the Bahamas and South Africa.

Apostle Roberson also founded an all-girls school in Pakistan. She has no regrets in answering the call of God; however, by no means has it been easy raising three sons, preaching, teaching, mentoring and traveling to different states and countries. Angela always finds time to pour into others and she is a woman of prayer, passion, and integrity. She often says that she could not do this without the presence and the power of God.

Her Journey:

As an Apostle of God, she officiated the Affirmation Service of two prophets —Spiritual Daughters (2025)

She has been featured in several covers of the *Gleaming Dreamers* Magazine

Influential Women to Know

Beyond the Break

She is a published author of Full Fledge "Understanding the power of faith"

She has co-authored two books to date:

- ✓ I am a Living Testimony, NO1 on Amazon (2025)
- ✓ Stronger, Better, Wiser "Walk into the New You"

She runs a mentorship programme at Compton High School (2022 to date)

She is also part of the co-team of the Faith in Blue with the Los Angeles Police Department (LAPD)

In 2024, she was awarded the MOU and buildings at Davey High School (Johannesburg, South Africa) to do mentorship programmes and other projects

In 2021, she was awarded appreciation for Outstanding Support to Passion to Love and Care Ministries, under the leadership of CEO Founder Prophetess Temika McCanns

In 2018, Award of Appreciation under Ministerial Alliance at City of Refuge

In 2017, she officiated the Affirmation Service (Prophet) of her spiritual daughter in Jamaica

In 2017–2019, she worked as a PR for Cross TV Network

In 2017, she earned her Bachelor's Degree in Biblical Studies and Counseling at Bible Believers College Seminary, graduating with Cum Laude

In 2017, she received the Award for Prayer at Bible Believers College Seminary

In 2016, she received the Humanitarian Award under the Ministerial Alliance at City of Refuge, under the leadership of Bishop Noel Jones

In 2016–now, she was a host of Prayer Saved My Life on the Cross TV Network

Cardiac Technician License acquired in 1993: Began working for LA County in 2000 as a Cardiac Technician in the Emergency Room at Harbor UCLA Medical Centre. Retired early in 2016

ARF Administration Development Disabled Adults acquired in 2007: Worked for Alondra Homes with level 4I clients between the year of 2008–2009. Also worked with various clients, including but not limited to the mentally ill, autistic, and disadvantaged children

However, her success does not stop there. Apostle Roberson has been the guest speaker of different local radio and international TV stations such as The Cross TV Network, OCN Broadcasting, KGLH Radio Station: Motherland Show, and K-Day FM Radio Station. She is also the author of *The Path of My Deliverance* and *Full Fledge: Understanding the Power of Faith.* She has also been featured in *Pastor S.L. Maxwell-Robles* Magazine

As impressive as Apostle Roberson's accolades sound, her love for God and His people are her drive and the focus of everything that she puts her on hands to do. She is a firm believer that promotion ONLY comes from God **(Psalm 75:6–7)**

Email: dktelevision7@gmail.com

Apostle Angela's Acknowledgments

Keisha George, your legacy is a testament to God's power and love.

Legacy & Commission

Rising, Influencing, and Finishing Strong

This is where it all comes together.

This final section lifts your gaze beyond yourself and into impact, influence, and legacy. These affirmations commission you to rise, to lead with love, and to walk boldly into the future God has prepared. You are not ending a book—you are being sent forward.

Rise Up! Together We Win

Affirmations for Faith, Love, and Divine Restoration
Affirmations by Ambassador Dr. Nephetina L. Serrano

I rise each day with divine purpose, guided by the Spirit of God.

Every morning is a divine appointment with destiny. The Word reminds us that "The steps of a good man are ordered by the Lord" (Psalm 37:23, NIV). When I wake, I align my heart with His will, knowing that I am not moved by circumstance but led by His plan. My purpose is not my own, it is born in the heart of God. I choose to move in obedience, trusting that, even in the unknown, He has already prepared the way. Each step I take is purpose-filled, anchored in faith, and destined to bring glory to His name.

I am equipped and empowered to restore what the enemy tried to destroy.

There is no broken place that God cannot rebuild. In relationships, families, and marriages, the power of restoration flows through obedience and grace. "The Lord will restore the years the locusts have eaten" (Joel 2:25, NIV). When I speak healing over what was lost, God breathes new life into every area that once seemed lifeless. I am His vessel of reconciliation, carrying light into dark spaces. I walk with spiritual authority, declaring that love wins, unity prevails, and every covenant God has ordained shall stand strong again.

I walk in divine confidence because my identity is rooted in Christ.

True confidence is not found in human validation but in divine revelation. I know who I am because I know Whose I am. The Word declares, "You are a chosen people, a royal priesthood, a holy nation, God's special possession" (1 Peter 2:9, NIV). My worth is not determined by titles or applause, it is sealed in the love of my Savior. When I face challenges, I do not shrink back in fear; I rise, clothed in divine boldness. Every assignment I carry is God-breathed and, through Him, I have the courage to fulfill it.

I am a vessel of love, bringing healing and unity wherever I go.

Love is the language of heaven and the heartbeat of purpose. "Above all, love each other deeply, because love covers over a multitude of sins" (1 Peter 4:8, NIV). I am called to embody the love of Christ in every conversation, in every act of service, and in every relationship. Where there is conflict, I bring peace. Where there is hurt, I bring compassion. Love is not weakness; it is divine strength that transforms hearts and restores trust. I choose to love like Christ, freely and without fear, because love never fails.

I am fearless in faith because I know God goes before me.

Faith does not deny fear, it conquers it. The Lord declares, "Be strong and courageous. Do not be afraid or discouraged, for the

Lord your God will be with you wherever you go" (Joshua 1:9, NIV). I refuse to let uncertainty silence my obedience. Even when I cannot see the full picture, I move forward in trust. Every battle before me is already won because my God fights for me. I stand in fearless faith, knowing that I am surrounded by divine favor and backed by the power of heaven.

I speak life because my words carry power and purpose.

The atmosphere responds to what I release. The Word teaches, "The tongue has the power of life and death, and those who love it will eat its fruit" (Proverbs 18:21, NIV). I choose to speak hope instead of fear, faith instead of doubt, and peace instead of chaos. My words create environments of victory, healing, and grace. As a leader and woman of purpose, I understand that every declaration shapes destiny. I will use my voice to uplift, to heal, and to remind others that God's promises never fail.

I am a light in the world, appointed to uplift and transform lives.

The call on my life is to shine. "You are the light of the world, like a city on a hill that cannot be hidden" (Matthew 5:14, NIV). My influence is not about recognition but revelation. I am positioned by God to impact lives, to speak truth, and to bring souls to the knowledge of His love. I carry light into places of darkness, bringing hope to the weary and restoration to the broken. Every word I speak and every action I take becomes a reflection of Christ within me. I will continue to rise, to serve, and to shine, because together we win.

Ambassador Dr. Nephetina L. Serrano

Ambassador Dr. Nephetina L. Serrano is a relationship expert, international speaker, counselor, evangelist, best-selling author, publisher, certified life coach, and mentor. She is the Co-Founder of Covenant Marriages, Inc., Covenant Rescue 911 501(c)(3), Covenant Marriages Institute, and *Marriage CEO Magazine*. As The Marriage CEO®, Dr. Serrano is a global voice for faith-based relationship restoration, empowerment, and leadership. Her humanitarian efforts have earned her numerous accolades, including the President's Lifetime Achievement Award (2021 and 2022) signed by President Joe Biden. Through her mission of love and restoration, she continues to strengthen families, empower leaders, and glorify God through every platform she touches.

Website: www.marriageCEOs360.com

Covenant Rescue 911 501(c)(3) - 24-Hour Hotline for Couples and Families in Crisis:

(855) RESC911 (737-2911) | (215) 550-1747

"RISE UP! TOGETHER WE WIN."

I Am The Vision Fulfilled

Affirmation by Dr. Kishma George

I am walking boldly in the vision God placed within me.

God has entrusted you with a vision that carries divine purpose and eternal impact. Walking boldly in that vision means refusing to let fear or uncertainty silence your faith. When you step forward in obedience, even without having all the answers, Heaven responds to your movement. Remember, "The steps of a good man are ordered by the Lord" (Psalm 37:23). You are not walking alone—God has already prepared the way. Each step of faith you take activates doors of destiny. Boldness is your weapon against hesitation and obedience is your key to manifestation.

I am divinely equipped for every assignment and season.

Every vision requires divine equipping and God has already provided you with the tools you need to succeed. Whether you are entering a new season or facing a difficult transition, remember that His grace is sufficient and His strength is made perfect in weakness (2 Corinthians 12:9). You don't need to compare your journey to anyone else's; your preparation is unique. Divine equipping means that wisdom, strategy, and supernatural favor are already aligned with your purpose. You are fully capable, qualified, and chosen for this very moment in time.

I am not waiting on the right moment; I am creating it with faith.

Faith is not passive—it is active and powerful. Many people wait for ideal circumstances before moving forward, but true visionaries understand that faith makes moments happen. Hebrews 11:1 reminds us that "faith is the substance of things hoped for, the evidence of things not seen." When you step out in faith, even with small beginnings, God meets your movement with miracles. Do not wait for external confirmation; move forward knowing Heaven has already approved your assignment. Your faith creates the moment your vision becomes reality.

I am becoming everything God spoke over my life.

Transformation is a divine process. You are not who you used to be and you are still becoming all that God destined you to be. Every challenge, test, and delay is shaping your character for the promise. God's Word declares, "Being confident of this very thing, that He which hath begun a good work in you will perform it" (Philippians 1:6). Trust the process. The becoming stage is where God refines, molds, and strengthens you for the manifestation of His Word. Embrace each season as a stepping stone toward your destiny.

I am a builder of dreams, nations, and generations.

You were never created to dream small. God has called you to be a builder—of ideas, families, ministries, and legacies. Just as Nehemiah rebuilt the walls of Jerusalem, you too are called to restore, renew, and raise up foundations for many generations (Isaiah 58:12). The dreams inside you are not only for you; they are divine blueprints for others to follow. As you build with faith, integrity, and purpose, your obedience becomes a bridge for future generations to cross into destiny.

I am unstoppable because God's hand is upon my life.

When God's hand is on your life, no force of opposition can halt your destiny. You are unstoppable—not because of your strength but because of His divine covering. Every setback is a setup for greater victory. Like Joseph, what others meant for harm God will turn for your good (Genesis 50:20). The anointing on your life gives you resilience to rise again after every fall. Keep your focus, remain steadfast, and know that Heaven's power is backing you. The unstoppable believer moves forward even in the face of impossibility.

I am a living testimony that God's vision always manifests in His perfect time.

Vision requires patience, faith, and endurance. God's promises are sure, and though the vision may tarry, it will come to pass at the appointed time (Habakkuk 2:3). You are a living testimony that delays are not denials. Every prayer, every tear, and every waiting season is working for your good. When you surrender to God's timing, you experience peace in the process and purpose in the pause. Rest in knowing that the vision is not just coming—it's maturing, unfolding, and aligning with divine timing.

Apostle Dr. Kishma A. George

Often described as a "Dream Pusher," Apostle Dr. Kishma A. George is a dynamic inspirational speaker, entrepreneur, mentor, playwright, TV host, radio personality, producer, and 19-time best-selling author. Her mission is clear: to inspire individuals to pursue and fulfill their God-given purpose—no matter their circumstances.

As the director of the *Women Destined for Greatness Mentoring Program* in Kent County, Delaware, Dr. George is dedicated to helping others recognize the greatness within them. She is also the visionary and editor-in-chief of *K.I.S.H. Magazine* and the founder, president and CEO of *K.I.S.H. Home, Inc. (Kingdom Investments in Single Hearts)*—an organization committed to transforming the lives of girls and women in Delaware, particularly those who are in or have aged out of foster care.

Her work with aged-out foster youth revealed the many challenges they face—homelessness, lack of financial literacy, low self-esteem, single parenthood, and limited access to support systems. As an independent living mentor, she witnessed their struggle to navigate adulthood while still in high school or without emotional and financial stability. Compelled to make a difference, Dr. George established a 24-hour transitional home in Delaware, offering young women a safe, supportive environment to grow, heal, and thrive. Her efforts continue to impact lives by promoting emotional resilience and economic independence.

Dr. George's dedication has been recognized in major publications such as the *Dover Post, Delaware News Journal, Delaware State News, Milford Beacon, Wisdom for Everyday Life, Kingdom Voices Magazine, Gospel 4 U Magazine, BOND Inc.*, and her own *K.I.S.H. Magazine*. She has also been featured on TV and radio programs including *Atlanta LIVE, Delmarva WBOC-ABC, Life Talk Radio Show, Straight Talk for Women Only, 101.7 FM, Fox Fire Radio*, and *The Frank and Travis Radio Show* on *Praise 105.1*.

Her numerous accolades include:

- ✓ **Woman of the Year for Entrepreneurial Success**, Empowered Women Ministries
- ✓ **Diversity Award**, State of Delaware/Social Services (2013)
- ✓ **Authentic Servant Leadership Award** (2014)
- ✓ **Outstanding Service Award**, DSU Alumni Association (2014)
- ✓ **Church Girlz Rock Humanitarian Award** (2015)
- ✓ **Faith Fighter Award** (2016)
- ✓ **CHOICES "Woman of the Year"** (2016)
- ✓ **Governor's Tribute Award**, State of Delaware (2016)
- ✓ **Business Woman of the Year** (2016, 2018)
- ✓ **Global Smashers Award** (2017)
- ✓ **I AM Baby Doll Global & Devorah Awards** (2018)
- ✓ **World-Changer Award** (2019)

- ✓ **I Am Fabulous & Phenomenal Woman Awards** (2019, 2022)
- ✓ **Mogul of the Month** (2020)
- ✓ **Woman of Influence Spot** (2020)
- ✓ **London UK Star Trailblazer Award** (2023)
- ✓ **Global Mentor on Another Level Award** (2023)
- ✓ **EMMI Leadership & Business Award** (2023)
- ✓ **Global World Changer Award** (2024)
- ✓ **Legacy Award** (2025)

Through every platform she touches, Dr. Kishma empowers others to activate their faith, embrace their calling, and step into the fullness of their destiny. She firmly believes that every individual has a divine assignment—and it is her passion to see them rise and walk boldly into it.

Contact Information

Website: www.kishmageorge.com

Email: info@kishmageorge.com

Phone: 302-401-1317

Social Media Outlets

* Facebook Group - Gleaming Dreamers

* Facebook- Kishma George

* IG- DrKishmageorge

* Clubhouse- @Awakenthedreamer

* TikTok - Kishma George

* X aka Twitter - Kishma George

Dr. Kishma George Acknowledgements

First and foremost, I want to give God all the glory and honor as He made this vision possible. I love You, Lord, with all my heart! In memory of my beloved father, Edmond Felix George; I am thankful for his encouragement and inspiring me to dream. To the best mother in the world, Novita Scatliffe-George; I thank you for your love, support, encouraging words and praying for me. Thank you for not giving up on me. I love you, Mom! To my wonderful daughter Kiniquá, I love you dearly. Thank you for your encouraging words, hugs and love. To my family; James, Raeisha, Christopher, Joshua, Seriah, Janisha and Kayla —thank you for supporting the vision with your prayers and love. A special thank you to the co-authors of the Write the Vision affirmation book. A special thank you to my beautiful Jackie Hicks for her amazing photography and the beautiful Letitia Thornhill for her gift of makeup artistry. Love you, ladies! To K.I.S.H. Home, Inc.'s board/advisors, volunteers and mentors; thank you for your dedication, support and believing in the vision of helping to make a difference in the lives of young women in Delaware. To Emily Ann Warren, thank you for your support, love, and believing in me. To Prophetess Ayanna, publisher; I thank God every day for bringing you into my life. You have been a blessing. Thank you for your encouraging words, support, love and believing in the vision. Love you Lastly, but not least, I would like to thank D›vine Designs and everyone who encouraged, prayed for and supported K.I.S.H. Home, Inc. over the years, I am forever grateful. God Bless!

Made in the USA
Coppell, TX
08 February 2026

70636061R00089